Wedding *of the* Foxes

Also by Katherine Larson

Radial Symmetry

Wedding

of the

Foxes

essays

Katherine Larson

MILKWEED EDITIONS

© 2025, Text by Katherine Larson
All rights reserved. No portion of this book may be used or reproduced for the training of artificial intelligence. Except for brief quotations in critical articles or reviews, no part of this book may be reproduced in any manner without prior written permission from the publisher: Milkweed Editions, 1011 Washington Avenue South, Suite 300, Minneapolis, Minnesota 55415.
(800) 520-6455
milkweed.org

Published 2025 by Milkweed Editions
Printed in Canada
Cover design by Mary Austin Speaker
Cover art by Utagawa Hiroshige, *New Year's Eve Foxfires at the Changing Tree, Ōji*, circa 1857; held by the Met—Rogers Fund, 1925
Author photo by Alex Thomé
25 26 27 28 29   5 4 3 2 1
First Edition

Library of Congress Cataloging-in-Publication Data

Names: Larson, Katherine, 1977- author.
Title: Wedding of the foxes : essays / Katherine Larson.
Description: First edition. | Minneapolis, Minnesota : Milkweed Editions, 2025. | Summary: "An elegant collection of lyric essays that embraces fractures, contradictions, and the interconnectedness of life on Earth"-- Provided by publisher.
Identifiers: LCCN 2024048279 (print) | LCCN 2024048280 (ebook) | ISBN 9781639550067 (paperback) | ISBN 9781639550074 (ebook)
Subjects: LCGFT: Essays.
Classification: LCC PS3612.A7736 W43 2025 (print) | LCC PS3612.A7736
 (ebook) | DDC 814/.6--dc23/eng/20250131
LC record available at https://lccn.loc.gov/2024048279
LC ebook record available at https://lccn.loc.gov/2024048280

Milkweed Editions is committed to ecological stewardship. We strive to align our book production practices with this principle, and to reduce the impact of our operations in the environment. We are a member of the Green Press Initiative, a nonprofit coalition of publishers, manufacturers, and authors working to protect the world's endangered forests and conserve natural resources. *Wedding of the Foxes* was printed on acid-free 100% postconsumer-waste paper by Friesens Corporation.

For Vivienne & Theo

Contents

Threshold: Compass and Mirror / 1

Kintsugi: Art of Repair / 11

Bamboo | *Kurahashi Yumiko* / 23

Gleaners / 29

Wedding of the Foxes / 39

Blue Horizon | *Tawada Yōko* / 51

Haunted Household Objects / 57

Seagulls | *Ōba Minako* / 67

The Crane Wife / 73

Broken Toy Party / 87

Mt. Fuji | *Ōta Yōko* / 91

Monarchs: Art of Grieving / 97

Phoenix | *Taeko Kōno* / 107

Microseasons: Selections / 115

Sea Creatures | *Tsushima Yūko* / 137

Soap: Art of Failure / 145

Gardens | *Shibaki Yoshiko* / 159

My Monster, Your Monster, Our Monster / 165

The Twilight World / 173

Additional Reading / 183

Acknowledgments / 185

Wedding *of the* Foxes

Threshold

COMPASS AND MIRROR

When the gulls started fighting, it was over the trash snarled in the harbor water—paper coffee cups and oil-slicked twigs tangled among Sprite bottles. I'd left my apartment on Rugby Road in the dark and arrived in Baltimore before the aquarium opened. The sun rose. I watched the gulls pick apart a bag of Doritos, the buildings parse the pink of the sky into glassy triangles. It was the kind of waiting that makes you feel like a grimy plate of glass being slowly squeegeed.

I'd driven through the early morning hours to see the seadragons. I'd never seen them before—not in person. Like their seahorse relatives, leafy seadragons are from the family Syngnathidae, whose members possess traits so unusual that Victorian naturalists and scientists, even as recently as the nineteenth century, found them difficult to classify. While seahorses possess prehensile tails, leafy seadragons are known for the leaflike skin filaments that embellish their serpentine bodies: hybrids of both plant and dragon.

When I first saw them, suspended in their aquarium, they looked like tiny, golden chandeliers of seaweed. Buoyant, impossibly delicate, they moved so languidly it was as if they swam through cooling glass. I stepped closer and the sound of the crowd withdrew. I felt as though a window had opened in my chest, and something had slipped inside, nudging past my sagging organs and depositing little pinprick sparks of electricity. I was no longer a self the way the seadragons were no longer creatures clasped in an aqueous cube. Something pulsed between and through us and even when I drove home a few hours later, the sky seemed impossibly larger and I still felt those invisible trailing tendrils unspooling over miles, linking their lives with mine.

•

Years passed, and those seadragons were mostly forgotten. One sweltering August, my partner and I were stranded in Cuba for two weeks when our airline went bankrupt. We flew back from Havana on a Russian plane with cigarette burns on the seats and exit signs written in Cyrillic. I started throwing up before I even got a positive pregnancy test. It happened quickly: One day I was collecting the rare books of a Cuban poet to translate; a week later I couldn't shower or dress myself without help. Hyperemesis gravidarum is a severe, pregnancy-long form of nausea and vomiting. I found myself suddenly afloat in the buzzing atmosphere of my body's molecule-level distress. I felt as though the self I knew was being sheared from me; what was left had to sink down, and become something else.

Time grew into a shadowy hand of erasure, relooping the text of each day at an anguishingly sluggish pace. I spent entire days in dark rooms with my eyes closed. Screens made me vomit, but sometimes I could read a little. In a winter issue of *Ploughshares*, I found the poem "The Leafy Sea-Dragon" by Miho Nonaka. Curled in a shadowed bedroom, I read this line: *Life makes a sea full / of superfluous things*. It made me remember what it was like to stand in the aquarium that day. To behold a creature so unfathomable it seemed an excess.

•

Contrary to popular thought, the leaflike appendages of leafy seadragons do not allow them to swim. Instead, a seadragon possesses two translucent fins—one on its back, another on the ridge of its neck—that allow it to maneuver. But often they simply drift, slipping through seawater like seaweed marionettes. There's a scientist from Western Australia who once spent three days following a leafy seadragon. It tumbled in the currents just like a clump of seagrass, a strand of kelp.

Taxonomists will tell you how difficult it is to identify seahorses; their coloration and skin texture can change dramatically. Leafy seadragons, too, are such masters of camouflage that scientists often find it easier to search for them at night. They can be many things at once; it's not a question of what species they are (there is only one), but rather, how many permutations of the same self they are capable of inhabiting.

•

After thirty-nine weeks and four days, our daughter was born and the hyperemesis ended. I ate two plates of limp hospital broccoli and couldn't stop crying. I was delirious with happiness, with the thrum of her newborn heart against my skin. I discovered I could shower and walk in the sunlight again. After a few months, I took her to the Tucson Botanical Gardens, where cactuses with names like powder puff and Mexican fire barrel waved their blossoms like they were throwing us a party. My favorite spot to sit was the Barrio Garden with its jumble of coffee-can succulents and glossy citrus and a shrine where people left their remembrances. A tiny white shoe, a crumpled wrist corsage, little winking milagro charms, a set of car keys. We walked in that place of miracles and strange and hybrid forms. My daughter felt like one of them.

But the slow erasure and transformation of parenthood is not for the faint of heart. When I first started reading Japanese literature, it was because I wanted to escape. To inhabit an unattainable space: the snow country, a room of gold lacquerware and shadows. A spare and elegant lyricism that had nothing to do with the daily chaos of my own domestic life—a colicky baby, an environmental crisis that was becoming clearer by the day, the patriarchal structures that had become even more glaringly apparent to me as a new mother, and the struggle between trying to honor the remarkable space of my daughter's early years and watching my working life languish. In those early days, I read the work of men—Kawabata Yasunari, Tanizaki Jun'ichirō, Akutagawa Ryūnosuke, and others because they were more translated and available.

We moved and moved again. I found myself collecting more and more books by Japanese writers. Abe Kōbō. Mishima Yukio. Shōno Junzō. I scrawled down sentences like this one from Ōe Kenzaburō's *A Personal Matter*: "Evening was deepening, and the fever of early summer, like the temperature of a dead giant, had dropped completely from the covering air." Many possessions were abandoned—coffee tables, china, houseplants—but books were carried from one house to the next like nesting materials.

When I got pregnant again, my daughter and I baked a cake for my partner and placed a small fève charm inside: a son. Another difficult pregnancy followed and then came to an end. The whiplash of those early years, sneaking chlorine-stained pages during swimming lessons and chapters by IKEA night-light with my son's baby snores against my chest. We hunkered down in a city with endless, sinus-freezing winters, and moved to another so densely populated you had to drive for an hour through nearly gridlocked traffic to reach a stinking, man-made lake. To find any semblance of the natural world, I turned again and again to Japanese writers. I built a room I could live in inside that literature, then a house. I existed both in a place of neon pink Play-Doh cookies and a space where sparrows foretold futures and a man traced his friend through successive reincarnations, each time trying to prevent his early death.

•

Leafy seadragons are both rare and fragile, one of the many marine species vulnerable to human impacts. If you step back from a spinning globe, their entire range—Kangaroo Island to Rottnest Island in Australia—could be covered by the span of a finger. They are under threat not only from aquarium hobbyists and the Asian traditional medicine trade but are highly susceptible to pollution, overfishing, and habitat loss. Storms of rising intensity can also have devastating effects: Leafy seadragons are often found washed up on beaches afterward, tangled in clumps of seaweeds and seagrass.

Life makes a sea full / of superfluous things. I also like those first lines of Miho Nonaka's poem because they illustrate a basic human instinct: to consider nonhuman life superfluous simply because one does not know anything about it, its connectivity, or entanglements. Or sometimes that it even exists.

•

Then I discovered the writing of Kurahashi Yumiko, Ōta Yōko, and other Japanese women writers. This time, it was like being given the key to an entirely different kind of house, one with a strangely mutable yet expansive view. They showed me the slugs sliding around the ruins of Hiroshima, the devastating dissociative grief that can emerge following the death of a child, and the sheer imaginative power that allows one to endure the social isolation of single parenthood and/or crippling domestic duties. Here were writers writing with, as the editors of *Japanese Women Writers: Twentieth Century Short Fiction* observe, "some of the most penetrating feminist perception, imagination, and thought of the age." Instead of escape, they led me deeper and pried me open. Even in this age of grief and extinction, I knew that I didn't want numbness or escape. I wanted to hear something that was calling inside me, to somehow unify broken and disjointed pieces, internal and external. To see what was there in the raw edges, the dissonances, the contradictions.

•

Charismatic megafauna is a term biologists use for species that are compelling to the general public—species like koalas or giant pandas—that capture their attention or imagination. This can be a source of frustration to those biologists studying more inconspicuous species or relationships. Humans are drawn to anthropomorphize. But they are also drawn to otherness, and experience and knowledge of otherness, like the Ancient Greek χάρισμα (chárisma)—precursor to to our modern word charisma—can be a "gift of grace." Though found more than eight thousand miles from my home in the Arizona desert, the leafy seadragon, like most other charismatic species, is under threat from human impacts. And like other "umbrella or flagship species," a single charismatic species can encourage people to learn more about the other inhabitants of their ecosystem as well as the threats to that ecosystem's survival.

•

"To create a compass," the Japanese writer Tawada Yōko says, "or just to sharpen one's means of orientation, it is useful, I believe, to fundamentally lose one's sense of direction at least once." She speaks of the possibilities inherent in exploring a body of literature that is not of your own culture, and how it allows one to become "at least partially reborn." She argues that one learns to observe the patterns in a foreign world with a kind of critical awareness and responsiveness while also being able to see one's own culture from a perceptive distance. This kind of "heightened consciousness," she says, "can lead to the creation of artworks that are compasses and mirrors."

I like that idea of compasses and mirrors—the words speak of both orientation and reflection. Both imply contemplation, the possibilities inherent in pause. For example, it was only when I had my children that I started to realize how many of the childhood stories my mother had read to me came from Japan: stories about a crane wife, about a woman who follows a lost dumpling into the crack of the earth and finds monsters, about a dragon king of the river and the giant centipede he needed help defeating. Had this literature shaped my ethical landscape? In the stories of the forests and the forest spirits, the sly foxes and badgers-turned-teapots? Was it partly this literature that had made me more sensitive to the more-than-human lives around me, even as a child?

•

Whether crafted of polished bronze or volcanic obsidian, mirrors in antiquity were considered precious. Though the Romans were the first to invent glass mirrors, Venetian mirror-makers used special mixtures of bronze and gold to create reflections more lustrous than reality. In Japan, mirrors were placed within Shintō shrines to converse with the gods. "We don't see things as they are, we see them as we are," says Anaïs Nin. What if a mirror is more than a tool of simple reflection: offering alternative possibilities, enlarging perception, and making clear hidden suffering? What if a mirror allowed a species to see, instead of only the self, the connection with others, to our threatened, twilight world? What if mirrors are leafy seadragons, monarch butterflies, and red-crowned cranes?

Compasses are meant to show direction and to help forge a new path if one realizes the course one has set is unsatisfactory or if one is simply lost. What if compasses are of many kinds, many varieties? My compasses became Ōba Minako, Tawada Yōko, Shibaki Yoshiko, Tsushima Yūko, and other Japanese women writers.

•

The lineage of colonialism is one of taking a piece of culture because it's useful to one's art or project. It is an act for the self, one that does not allow the contemplation of consequences or harm. An act of cultural exchange, in contrast, is one in which an artist is not only fundamentally working from a place of care and sensitivity to these consequences, but working with the aim of giving back something to that community—a reciprocity.

"This entangled quality of life on Earth," Deborah Bird Rose tells us, "depends on and supports connectivity. There are numerous ways into thinking about these matters. I offer one way: the kinship mode. It situates us here on Earth, and asserts that we are not alone in time or place: We are at home where our kind of life (Earth life) came into being, and we are members of entangled generations of Earth life, generations that succeed each other in time and place." It's the entangled places I feel most drawn to: motherhood and monster stories, Japanese literature and the stark reality of this sixth extinction we are currently experiencing. I want to find—and make—compasses and mirrors that allow me to be capable of a different kind of receptivity and insight.

•

The leafy seadragon is sinuous and supple like the dragons of East Asian legend. Such dragons were thought to be able to control bodies of water—rivers, lakes, seas—as well as the weather. In times of prolonged drought, Buddhist monks recited sutras to encourage the dragon king—a rain dragon thought to live in a pond at the Shinsen-en or "Divine Spring Garden" in Kyōto—to rise from the pond and deliver a storm. I like the thought that improbable things can become reality. That a seadragon can exist as both tangible fact and myth.

The second time I saw leafy seadragons was at the Oceanário de Lisboa aquarium with my family. After we spent hours walking through the aquarium, we decided, instead of leaving, to start at the beginning and walk through the entire aquarium again. Our son wanted to return to the axolotls, our daughter, the cuttlefish. After walking once more through the leafy seadragon exhibit, I took a picture of a poem by Portuguese poet Sophia de Mello Breyner Andresen that had been etched on the wall. Later, my friend sent this translation:

> At the bottom of the sea there are white terrors
> Where plants are animals
> And animals are flowers.

Kintsugi

ART OF REPAIR

THE STORY BEGINS WITH A TEABOWL THAT WAS shattered. When fifteenth-century shōgun Ashikaga Yoshimasa sent his beloved broken teabowl away to be repaired, he was disappointed to find the teabowl returned with mended seams of ugly metal staples. According to historians, it was more than disappointment. He found this solution unacceptable.

"I'm not trying to be difficult," the sunburnt teenager squinted, standing in front of the juvenile fin whale skeleton. "But I just don't see why it matters." She looked at the teenager, a ponytailed brunette chewing a hangnail. The heat was ferocious, the tiny creases of her eyelids stung with sweat. This was at the end of the free natural history talk she gave on Sundays at the field station in the northern Gulf of Mexico, after she'd explained the homologous structures of the whale flipper and human arm. "Look here," she'd gestured to the wooden paddle fixed on the side of the fin whale rib cage (its arches towering above her head). "See how alike they are." The whale phalanges—stuck through with metal pins—were strewn against the salt-swollen wood like a cupful of dice.

Ashikaga challenged his craftsmen to find a new form of restoration. So they pulled out the staples. Painstakingly mended the seams with layers of tree sap dusted with gold.

In this talk, she'd been describing species that were threatened or endangered. Whale species and, in particular, the vaquita, a small endemic porpoise on the verge of extinction. "Suppose," the teenager had continued, "we didn't know they existed—if we were unaware of them completely, would it matter, really, if we lost them?" The teenager doesn't say this flippantly but with a kind of bleary bewilderment. It is the kind of terrifying question—both the significance and the explanation of it—that she will spend her life trying to come to terms with.

The teabowl was again returned to Ashikaga and the art of kintsugi, or "golden joinery," was born. Each piece unique, not in spite of, but because of the way it was both broken and repaired.

She must have said something to the girl in response, something stark and brittle, though now she doesn't remember. She remembers instead what she wanted to say: The world is full of secret and invisible machinery, our expression and understanding of which are utterly inadequate. She feels them, of course. Those threads that link the vaquita to the hedgehog cactus at her feet that's tossing its fuchsia blossoms at the sun. The threads that tie herself to this strange girl asking her a question she feels entirely unprepared to answer. She's felt them tug at her since she was small.

•

When she thinks of her time at the field station now, she remembers how she used to drag a thin sleeping mat out onto the porch to sleep. And of the picnic table that held the objects she used for her natural history talks—the fragile ones the children loved to stroke with their fingertips: the sea lion and bottlenose dolphin skulls, the seaweedish-looking egg cases of sharks and rays, the life-sized model of the small porpoise that was quickly becoming a ghost. That particular sound of the palms that shook their fronds at night while the ocean chewed its way up and down the shore.

The Sengoku period of Japan—when the art of kintsugi flourished—is noted as a time of near-constant civil war and social and political upheaval. It was also marked by several devastating earthquakes. Japan straddles multiple fault lines with the densest seismic network in the world. Fractures are part of its elemental substrate.

Her friend HG is making plaster casts of estuary mud from the sea where they met. Recording creatures that have passed, capturing transient marks that will be erased with the incoming tide. This feels to her an apt metaphor—that the change can be nearly imperceptible yet all-encompassing. How we may inhabit a new kind of being or expanse yet, in a moment, be brought back to selves that we have left behind or outright discarded. Like standing in a room of broken statuary. Rows upon rows of frozen objects, some of them truncated, maimed. Some of them still scraping their way across the floor. *If we can't leave those selves behind*, she thinks, *how do we integrate them?* She thinks about her own selves. The *she* that is the third-person excavator of memory's shifting constellations; the *I* that writes letters at night to Japanese authors she'll never meet.

In *Arts of Living on a Damaged Planet*, the authors explain, "The winds of the Anthropocene carry ghosts—the vestiges and signs of past ways of life still charged in the present. [. . .] Our ghosts are the traces of more-than-human histories through which ecologies are made and unmade." She is reminded one day on a walk with her children that the mourning dove eggshell they have found could be thought of as another smaller, intimate teabowl.

According to Kyōto kintsugi practitioner Kiyokawa Hiroki, "The fractured part where kintsugi is applied becomes a new landscape in itself." In this landscape, an artifact's unique history is honored. "Our imperfections," he says, "can be the birth of something new." There are times that this metaphor seems almost like a living thing to her—a cipher to be captured and held close like a rare and lovely moth. And then there are times when she finds toilet paper piled up so high inside the toilet bowl it resembles a wedding cake, and her pockets are full of mangy gift-feathers and Band-Aid wrappers, and while she's brushing the children's teeth, there's a voice inside of her that's sobbing and little fragments of poetry burning in incandescent images that she can't decipher, much less write down. There are times during the COVID-19 pandemic that she falls asleep in her clothes for the fourth night in a row.

Carlo Rovelli, the Italian physicist, argues that a human being is not a being at all, but a process, "like a cloud above the mountains." This echoes the Buddhist idea that there is, in fact, no permanent self to cling to. What's the difference between the self and a ghost?

•

She remembers one day at the field station when a pickup truck pulled up. A Mexican government official had confiscated the carapaces of sea turtles—he didn't say from where. "I didn't know where else to take them," he said. "I thought you could use them to teach." She remembers what it felt like as she helped unload them from the truck. It was like standing there watching someone cut the throat of an elephant. There are seven species of sea turtles. Six are counted as threatened or endangered. Most of the carapaces were still spongy in places where they hadn't been scraped clean of meat. The smell of mute, rotting things. Flies all around.

"Grief is a path to understanding entangled shared living and dying," Donna Haraway tells us. "Human beings must grieve with, because we are in and of this fabric of undoing. Without sustained remembrance, we cannot learn to live with ghosts and so cannot think." Sometimes when the house is very quiet at night, empty of the sounds of young children, she thinks about the ghosts of things. The ghosts of previous selves. The future ghosts of birds.

The methods of repair fall into three distinct categories:

> *Crack*, the use of gold dust and resin or lacquer to link broken pieces, usually appearing as a running vein or seam of gold.
>
> *Piece method*, where the shape of a missing fragment is filled in completely with gold or a gold and lacquer compound.
>
> *Joint-call*, where a nonmatching ceramic fragment of a similar shape replaces the missing fragment of the original vessel, giving the vessel a "patchwork" look.

When teaching her students poetic forms in graduate school, she realized how little she understood about the nuances of haiku. The skill of their compression, the "kireji" (cutting word), the punning, the symbolic sophistication of seasonal references. She studied them. Then haibun, tanka, renga, sedoka, haikai. Fiction writers followed: Ōe and Kawabata; Abe, Tanizaki. Decades of her life steeped in Japanese writers and metaphors. Literature—and this is not an exaggeration—that has kept her afloat. She thinks of Deborah Bird Rose exploring the idea of "reciprocal capture." Rose says, "For philosopher Isabelle Stengers, 'reciprocal capture,' is 'an event, the production of new, immanent modes of existence' in which neither entity transcends the other or forces the other to bow down. It is a process of encounter and transformation [. . .]."

Because of the pandemic, she teaches her daughter, a fourth grader, about tropical rainforests and other biomes at home. But between the words ecology and mutualism and symbiosis, other words creep in. Deforestation, habitat fragmentation, sea level rise, ecocide, ecocatastrophe. Her daughter builds a rainforest habitat out of a small cardboard box. Makes bromeliads from tiny scraps of tissue paper and cuts out a three-toed sloth to hang on a vine. In her report, she writes, *The beaks of adult toucans can be blue, orange, yellow, green, fuchsia, and white. They are like living forest rainbows.* Her daughter tells her that during mating season, certain toucans toss fruit back and forth as a courtship ritual.

It's been asked: Did the life of the bowl begin once it was shattered? She doesn't particularly like easy metaphors for suffering. Finds it quietly abhorrent when people speak of being "enlarged by suffering" or "given the opportunity for suffering's gifts: empathy, sensitivity to the pain of others, a sense that impermanence means we must live deeply, and not anesthetized." Not because it isn't true but because it seems reductive. What she loves is metaphor that contains space for both insight and the inscrutable. You can say, for example, that history must be recognized in a way that gives the breakage meaning. You can say that beauty can be made more whole. Or you can say that a whale is a mirror above treetops. The self is a kingdom of air.

•

When she was pregnant and so sick she spent months broken on the tiles of the bathroom floor she read, sentence by single sentence and with terrible clarity, Mishima Yukio's *Sea of Fertility* tetralogy. Some of the loneliest books she's ever lived. She remembers having to lie down on the floor the one time she went to

Target to try to buy maternity clothes. Under a wall of enormous bras. The carpet—a palpitating blue—was stained with something indescribably filthy. Her partner had to leave her there to find a wheelchair. Most days, she couldn't shower without help. Most days, she couldn't stand without help.

Another story of the beginning of kintsugi mentions a bowl that was shattered, and a clever guest, Hosokawa Yūsai, knowing the host's hot temper, quickly intervened by improvising a poem about the bowl whose deftness dispelled the host's dark mood. Language was a part of the mending. Even now, this story is a part of the mending. Mending is a thing that continues.

Discovering Japanese women writers was another revelation. Enchi Fumiko, Miyamoto Yuriko, Nogami Yaeko, Uno Chiyo. Notice that she's writing their full names and didn't with the others. She hadn't realized how underrepresented they were—if she'd talked to someone that happened to have read Kawabata, they wouldn't know Sakiyama Tami, Nogami Yaeko, or Ozaki Midori. She began to dream of writing a book in which small fragments of certain stories could slip in. Not in her voice. But more like joint-call pieces. As the writers themselves had written them.

Vulnerability. Mistakes. The history of what's been broken and how we managed or didn't manage to mend it. The word nagori can be translated as "remnant, traces, memory." In those last two weeks of October, the nagori-no-chaji tea ceremony in which the mended objects are not just displayed, but used, involves savoring the last tea leaves collected the previous November. It is a time to let go, to enter the sadness of passing even as one recognizes the old season must die before the new one begins. To live alongside ghosts is to live in recognition of their warning. And in honor of their remembrance.

If she hadn't been in the police station filing the paperwork for her stalker. If the officer hadn't shown her the stack of papers that was a single night's domestic violence calls—many of them repeats, she was warned. If she hadn't decided then and dragged her mattress down the street to the dumpster in the middle of the night to dump illegally because it was too stained with cat pee to give to anyone. If she hadn't had to drive across the country and into another to get as far away as possible. She would have never arrived at the field station. She would have never started this life. This self would have become a different self.

•

She met her friend HG in that country of whale bones and palms. HG had driven to the field station as part of a project to clean the curio cabinets and set them up as an educational exhibit. Together, they pulled black widows and their messy webs out of the cavernous spaces. Hung mako shark jaws against the wall. When they sat for a break at the picnic tables in the courtyard, the ones where the sea wind gusts through, they noticed a jumping spider. It followed their conversation, swiveling its head when each of them spoke, as if listening in. They would remember it always as a sign. Like being inducted into the secrets of the ruins at Delphi.

Chanoyu, or "Way of Tea," practitioner Christy Bartlett explains, "Mended ceramics foremost convey a sense of the passage of time. The vicissitudes of existence over time, to which all humans are susceptible, could not be clearer than in the breaks, the knocks, and the shattering to which ceramic ware too is subject. This poignancy or aesthetic of existence has been known in Japan as mono no aware, a compassionate sensitivity, an empathetic compassion for, or perhaps identification with, beings outside oneself."

She thinks of how it's an invisible language, the language of species. When one studies ecology, one studies relationships between living and nonliving things. What it meant to her was that one studies the invisible in order to make it more visible. The astonishment of which she sometimes has to hide. Like the time in her botany class when the TA chastised her poetic language. He'd circled the phrases with red ink, explaining that a lab report was no place to describe that under the microscope the chloroplasts had seemed to tumble around like green, sentient pearls.

She's been teaching her daughter haiku: Matsuo Bashō and Kobayashi Issa. Still, she is startled when one late night she reads this haiku of Katō Shūson:

> *I kill an ant*
> *and realize my three children*
> *have been watching.*

She, too, feels inexplicably ashamed.

Items for the nagori-no-chaji tea ceremony are carefully curated. To drink from a bowl that has been cared for by another is to recognize a lineage to which one belongs. To recognize in a single moment both rupture and continuity. Inheritance.

Her favorite is a teabowl from the eighteenth century. Arita ware. A joint-call where a fragment of a bird from another teabowl has been spliced into the broken section of the bird of another. When she looks at the fragile veins of gold that mend that joining, she thinks of words like palimpsest. She thinks of breakage and repair as the intimate history of an object. Sometimes, she thinks of her own body as a bird's.

This is not just metaphor—one of the genes involved in human language has a homolog in the song genes of certain birds. We share DNA in common with zebra finches, sea urchins, daffodils.

•

Her daughter has broken her favorite pot: one with hand-drawn marks that look like waves. For a while, she keeps the pieces in a little pile above the washing machine. There are kintsugi kits one can buy off the internet, but one morning, after looking at the pieces, so many pieces, she takes the pieces outside and throws them in the trash. She almost immediately regrets the decision, and as she stands there with her wild hair and ratty pajamas (her neighbors always seem to catch her in her ratty pajamas) she thinks she could do it—she could be that crazy person who empties out and then digs through her entire trash and finds each piece—but the whole thing has an air of finality, of something that's already been unequivocally and quietly decided, and even though she knows that she will likely regret it, she walks back to the house instead.

As a child, she was terrified of fire. Of the house beginning to burn as she slept. That she would wake trapped in flames, hearing the screams of her family—she couldn't make it out of the fire to reach them. She'd lie awake in darkness that felt malignant, felt it skim her body like oil. Even at the time, it embarrassed her to have such a secret, dramatic anxiety. In her family, drama was frowned upon. They were pragmatists and stoics. They were not burning alive in lakes of fire.

And yet. Once she woke and the house was filled with the smell of smoke. When she screamed, her father came crashing from the bedroom and into the kitchen. On the stove was a pot of bones her mother had left on low heat, wanting to sterilize before giving them to the dog. The smell of singed bones: like having your lungs stuffed full of burnt sand.

Collectors became so enamored of the art form that some were accused of deliberately smashing valuable pottery so that it might be repaired with golden seams. Were there ever pieces that once broken, they realized they could not mend? There must have been.

She wants to believe that the extinction crisis can be slowed, halted. She wants to believe that something can be born out of it that does not negate the understanding of the damage that's already been done. Yet she secretly fears the tipping point at which the cascade will produce an uncontrollable unraveling.

They say some of the teabowls would simply fall apart and then again be remade. Those many hands, those many ghosts, those many years.

•

"We have never been individuals," biologist Scott Gilbert tells us. "If most of the cells in the human body are microbes, which 'individual' are we? We can't segregate our species nor claim distinctive status—as a body, a genome, or an immune system. And what if evolution selects for relations among species rather than 'individuals'?" She thinks again of the golden threads. Of entanglements. She thinks of her nine-year-old daughter's haiku:

> *Raindrops so shiny,*
> *And delicate on pavement*
> *The worms and snails slide.*

Bartlett says, "One of the most deeply held values in the tearoom is that of collaboration, of multiple hands producing a seamless whole in which each individual contributor still remains distinct. [...] In this bowl, we can see the hand of two artists, the original potter and the later lacquerer who brought [...] remarkable sensibility to the way in which the repair is highlighted." The plaster casts HG is making contain the tracks of hermit crabs, shorebirds, waves.

Maybe that golden thread of repair reminded Ashikaga of a river. Or the asymmetrical silhouette of a leaning mountain. Whatever it was, in its gold-seamed brokenness, Ashikaga found he loved the teabowl differently—more deeply than he had before.

When she teaches her daughter about mollusks, she shows her a video of the tiny blue orbs that line the edge of a living scallop. "Most people don't know," she says, "that scallops have eyes." And later, with her son at the tide pools she used to wade into drinking her morning coffee, in whose hand she places a still-dripping clam. "Or that Venus clams have nervous systems. Hearts."

Bamboo

KURAHASHI YUMIKO

Dear Kurahashi Yumiko,

It's been raining for several days now, and even the leafcutter ants' burrow is soggy with wilted blossoms and soaked leaves. The dampness clings—to our clothes, to the little hairs on the napes of our necks—in an exhalation of cloud that, at this very moment, I want to disappear in. The cat—dewy plant-lover—is currently vomiting grass under the kitchen table. My son has spent two hours waging a whine campaign whose sole purpose is to erode my resistance to buying him a Nerf grenade. And just last week, I shattered my bamboo teapot by knocking it to the floor with the laundry basket because we live in a "historic" house where the only sensible place to put the washing machine is in the kitchen. If I had my teapot, I'd make some tea, hunch over your stories, and think about everything I want to know.

I want to know things like what you read to get yourself through the days when your dentist father demanded that you attend dental hygiene school. And what it felt like to ditch being a dental hygienist to study French literature—your first memories of reading Valéry and Sartre and Rimbaud. I want to know what's meant when these lines are slipped into your biography: "despite significant health problems—" Were they talking about your sluggish heart or something else? And why did you refuse the operations? Did you feel like I do sometimes, that you've wasted not just hours of your life but *your very life* on words that won't matter to anyone? And if you did, I want you to know that this body, my body, has carried your stories while I heaved sparkling grapefruit water into my cart at Trader Joe's and quizzed my daughter on regular German verb conjugations and swept up the scattered litter around the litterbox—and that the stories have felt like a secret curtain in an ordinary room, behind which something extraordinary and diaphanous undulates, like light, but light that's alive.

Permeability—it's what I associate with your work. Like in your story "The Monastery" when the narrator says, "We walked behind the old abandoned belfry and took a small path that twisted and turned like a labyrinth through the grove. We seemed to be following the tracks of time, spiraling down into the interior of our spirits. Despite the encroaching heat, the grove had trapped cool, green air in its web of foliage. We wandered along the wooded path, avoiding the menacing sun which shone like an old bronze dish above us. [. . .] We entered a wood of cedars rising perpendicularly. Hundreds of parallel shafts of sunlight streamed through the trees to pierce our bodies." That coolness! That grove in which something refreshing thrums and vibrates! When I read those lines, it's like I can feel something in the depths of me exhale.

I bought a teapot yesterday at the local St. Vincent de Paul thrift store. And though I saw it months ago and recognized it immediately as Ōbori-sōma ware produced in the Fukushima Prefecture, I didn't buy it then. It was a deep green color, but with its gloss and scrolled gold (I realized later were horses, revered by the Sōma clan), it seemed, I don't know, too fancy. But when I happened to return to that part of the city after having breakfast with a friend, it was still there—except some of the set was now missing, and some of the teacups had been chipped. I couldn't stand it: seeing a beautiful thing left unloved and unwanted. At the time, I'd been reading more of your stories, and the color green stood out in my mind—that particular teapot color, too, something of a cross between sargassum seaweed and the sage-green shrubbery that dots the rocky badlands of Arizona's Painted Desert. There was another thing that struck me too: It's the only kind of porcelain I've seen that has a double wall, and what seemed particularly symbolic is that I know this because, near the bottom of the cup, three hearts are punched through that first layer, with a beautiful brushstroke wave painted beneath. Now I trace my fingertips against those openings and think of the moments when something or someone manages to find its way in.

When I read your stories, it's not just the body's permeability I think of, but the mind's as well. Your images swarm into my brain with tiny glittering hooks. The way in "To Die at the Estuary," weary women would visit a particular haunted pine grove, and "ghosts would appear in every tree in the form of a human head larger than you could put your arms around, and they would dangle there giving off a sulphurous light, crying together, calling." Doesn't it change things to think of forests not just as a group of trees but as repositories of ghosts, places of encounter?

What I love about your work is that it reminds me that sometimes the point is not to figure out the strangeness but instead simply not to turn away from it. And to see, perhaps, if you can even move closer. Not necessarily blindly or boldly, but with a kind of inquisitiveness that comes with recognizing how wildly peculiar the world really is and how little we actually know of it.

After all, we never know what may happen to knock us sideways out of our usual orbits. The way my eighty-year-old neighbor, MW, invited my family in to see her "Christmas Village"—what one might expect with both season and phrase: tables of tiny illuminated porcelain houses, tufts of polyester snow and snow-dusted bottlebrush trees, even a glossed cathedral and Walmart. And then some new intimacy in the conversation opened and—you would have loved this—she asked us if she could give us a tour of her "Elvis Room." The "Elvis Room" turned out to be an entire bedroom lavished with Elvis clocks and velvet paintings and china figurines and a framed skirt with Elvis printed on it that her aunt had made for her when she was fourteen. That Elvis room—it was magical.

You've taught me that permeability is about recognizing our rich entanglements with other lives. It's about understanding the boundaries between things are fundamentally blurry and being willing to take a risk so that something we may otherwise miss might be allowed in.

In fundamental ways, it's also about the creative power of resilience. I may now have to read your work with tea brewed in a different teapot. But I still remember your grove of bamboo and how bamboo itself was the first plant to regrow in the ruins of Hiroshima.

I like that so many of your stories are about getting lost because getting lost engenders its own kind of permeability. Sometimes, we have to do something different so we can finally learn to inhabit the world without all our hard armor again. And sometimes that learning comes only when something awful has happened and we must choose to walk forward through rooms of terrible pain simply because we believe there must be other unexpected possibilities on the other side, the faint outlines of doors that can lead to rooms we haven't yet imagined.

I remember camping on an island in the Queen Charlotte Sound, on a trip to record data on the summer feeding patterns of gray whales. I had hiked that afternoon and, in my tent, felt the familiar, ordinary exhaustion of fieldwork—sunburnt lips, waterlogged blisters from perpetually soggy boots, the sweaty fish-smell of my sleeping bag. But something else—the letter from a longtime love that I somehow knew as I held it meant the end. Too weary to care about dinner, I pitched early toward sleep. But then, the next morning, I woke earlier than the others. As if a voice had spoken: "Wake up, wake up, everything's ready, we're waiting for you." I didn't walk toward the sea; I walked inland, away from the shore.

Because of the fog, even the giant Sitka spruces seemed to be floating. And when the first rays of sunlight burned through, I saw something glisten close to the dirt. I'd only ever seen pictures, but I remembered them clearly from a book on carnivorous plants I'd checked out from the library as a girl. Sundew plants. Except I couldn't have imagined how tiny and jewellike they were. The ground was marshy, and I had to crouch. But I spent the first hour of that day watching sundews hunting.

So when I read your sentence, "hundreds of parallel shafts of sunlight streamed through the trees to pierce our bodies," I wonder—maybe it wasn't just light entering the body, but shining out of it too.

> With gratitude and admiration,
> Katherine

Gleaners

What delights her about Tanizaki's *In Praise of Shadows*, the first time she reads it, is the way he describes disliking things that shine. He "prefer[s] a pensive luster to a shallow brilliance. A murky light that, whether in a stone or artifact, bespeaks a sheen of antiquity. Of course," he continues, "this 'sheen of antiquity' of which we hear so much is in fact the glow of grime."

Each time she enters a thrift store she thinks of Agnès Varda's *The Gleaners and I*. The way the gleaners comb through fields and urban centers, salvaging vegetables, broken objects, furniture. It calms her to sift through the detritus for something beautiful that has been overlooked, cast away. Art deco letter holders, a blue morpho butterfly encased in glass. A box of cocktail parasols that make her improbably cheerful.

She discovered it was a way to get out of the house while soothing the tiny, colicky baby. A place where the baby would fall silent in the stream of objects under fluorescent light. (A window in her mind would open, and she could think again.) She'd wander through the aisles while the baby slept against her chest, lifting dish after dish of mismatched Nippon porcelain—candy bowl, cake plate, chipped teacup.

Tanizaki again: "For better or worse we love things that bear the marks of grime, soot, and weather, and we love the colors and the sheen that call to mind the past that made them. Living [. . .] among these old objects is in some mysterious way a source of peace and repose."

She loved Tanizaki's book because he reminded her that radiance was not radiance without history and contrast. He understood that one could not amputate the present moment from the past. Or, for that matter, from the future either.

At the thrift stores, she liked to touch things. Run her fingers over them. Vintage spoons, brass midcentury planters still clotted with dirt. A bag of unused popsicle sticks.

These places are repositories, she thinks, *of objects from those that have passed beyond*. The dumping grounds for family members left behind—the objects they do not wish to carry. Secretly, she loves this. Secretly, she sometimes imagines she stands in these places, like a beach at the end of the world, where the last items are washed up by the ocean from those who have stepped into the sky.

•

There were so many vintage Japanese teapots she began to collect them. White porcelain with hand-painted puffer fishes and scallops. Chrysanthemums etched in gold. Stoneware, lusterware, moriage. Some she saw over and over again. As if they'd been reincarnated. As if they had a message for her.

She wants to be clear: She's humbled by the centuries-old practice of the Japanese tea ceremony. Appreciates the history, the sophisticated nuance, the cultural significance. Understands this is not her practice. When she talks about making tea, she's talking about her attempt to embrace the constraints of her current life. To make some tea and edit her student's thesis and steal a few pages of a Tawada Yōko novel while the baby is napping. Or to put it bluntly—a lot of mess and breakage and little space for contemplation. Especially the quiet, uninterrupted kind.

But still, it delights her to steep tea in those teapots. With their histories and former lives. She thinks of the moment in Kawabata's *Thousand Cranes* when the protagonist uses a three-hundred-year-old Shino teabowl as a vase for freshly cut flowers. That juxtaposition of aesthetics: Life is fleeting. The object remains.

Of course, it's not all poetic. That's partly the point. It's true that the thrift stores were sometimes rather grimy places. Water stains in the ceilings. Weary shoppers. Stained bras, ratty stuffed animals. The shuffled feet and downcast eyes. The shouting flurry when a shoplifter slipped out of the store, or the breaking of dishes. But even that seemed like something she belonged to, a part of the patina.

The thrift store in Fairfax, Virginia, reminded her of living in Mexico. The pine oil smell of Fabuloso cleaner. Little bodegas at the front of the store playing *Luz de Luna* and *Mariachi Vargas de Tecalitlán*. Rows of cell phones and colored lights and the vivid primary-colored plastic of children's toys. She got good at finding what they needed. Those years living on a postdoc stipend, the anxious checking of the bank account each day for overdrafts.

And she had to get out of the house, craved sanctuary with other women. The grandmothers were her favorite. Russian, Persian, Japanese, Ukrainian, Colombian—they cooed over her son and spoke to him with gestures of their hands.

At birth, her son had been rushed to the NICU. Some things resolved, but his reflux remained, severe enough to stop his breathing. The solution: a strict diet for herself and breastfeeding every two hours around the clock for a year. She remembers being so sleep-deprived that her ears would ring, and the walls would wrap around her and spin as if she were drunk and had just stepped off a merry-go-round.

She thought of that place in the hospital as The Bird Room. Because she dreamed that her son was a baby bird that dissolved in her hands like raw hamburger. And because she kept remembering the main character of Ōe Kenzaburō's novel *A Personal Matter*—also named Bird—and the traumatic birth of his own son.

Those flashbacks—the news of the suicide bombers in Paris, her son in the NICU's clear plastic box, alarms going off when he had another episode of apnea—sent such a wave of panic through her body that she didn't dare try to find another solution. It seemed a small price to pay. (Upon reflection, this perhaps wasn't the most helpful perspective; it nearly cost her her sanity.) But she knew there were others; she'd held them, sobbing. She'd glimpsed what it meant that her bird had made it out of The Bird Room alive.

•

She goes to the thrift store because she feels anonymous. Because it feels like a kind of meditation to sift through damaged, discarded things. Though she never really wants to run into anyone she knows.

Sometimes she disliked the almost clinical cleanliness of T.J. Maxx and HomeGoods. Not just the way that objects felt identical, remnants of mass production. But the gloss of their newness. She wanted things around her that connected her life to other lives.

This compulsion toward invisible connection was not new. In college, she'd studied ecology and evolutionary biology. That, too, was the study of invisible connections. Things that arrived at the very edges of perception. Relationships often unnoticed and unseen.

How phosphorous from Saharan dust is blown across the ocean to feed the Amazonian rainforest. How leaves that fall into streams leach acids that fuel plankton growth in oceans. How spawning in a species of deep-sea sea urchin coincides with the new moon. How the iridescent cells in giant clams filter wavelengths of light most beneficial for their algae symbionts. How the messy roots of mangroves provide a necessary nursery for young lemon sharks.

Tanizaki says, "The quality that we call beauty [. . .] must always grow from the realities of life [. . .]." This is what she loved about science. It was never something to be arrived at. It opened continuously; it didn't end.

This was another aspect of the thrift store. It was a place of chance, of surprise. When so many aspects of existence tended toward confirmation biases, this was a way to stumble upon something unusual: vintage games, porcelain parrots. Prints from long-forgotten artists. A miniature puzzle of Picasso's *Guernica*. A tiny replica of an Incan temple her daughter builds, then glues on little scraps from a bag of dried moss.

There's a Japanese expression, hakidame ni tsuru, or "crane on the rubbish heap," which means a thing of beauty or elegance found in an unlikely place.

And books! Books on flower origami, glow-in-the-dark animals, and motherboard component repair. She loved the dog-eared books of poetry, books with postcards left as bookmarks: the coffee-stained Colosseum, handwritten notes: "I've arrived!" or "Tonight we're going to have a marshmallow roast on the beach."

She'd look for books she loved and scan their pages for marginalia. It was like listening in on a conversation. The last pages of E. M. Forster's *Where Angels Fear to Tread*, for example. That agonizing scene between Philip and Miss Abbott—and their rushing back through the carriage to close the window so the smut won't get into Harriet's eye. Though these were never books she'd buy; the voices broke her concentration. But in the thrift store, she wanted to hear them. She listened.

And the other book lovers delighted her too. Floating through the book section with piles of books in their arms. Triumphant as some of Varda's gleaners with their treasures.

Varda says, "I'm interested in people who are not exactly the middle way, or who are trying something else because they cannot prevent themselves from being different, or they wish to be different, or they are different because society pushed them away." There's a scene in *The Gleaners and I* where Varda collects heart-shaped potatoes—discarded for their perceived imperfection—out of the piles left in the fields.

It wasn't just the thrill of finding a deal. Or sifting through ruins for lost and forgotten fragments. It was the sense of turning away from an obsession with the new, and with the careless discarding. That sense of looking more closely at familiar, quieter places. Finding something in that ugliness, the humbling everyday banality.

Tanizaki says, "Such is our way of thinking—we find beauty not in the thing itself but in the patterns of shadows, the light and the darkness, that one thing against another creates."

•

Here's the truth: Most of the time, it feels like her life is composed of skating across surfaces. Shiny constructions of the self. She craves the things that are beneath the surfaces. The real that she senses is through and inside and around them.

After Varda died, heart-shaped potatoes were left outside her home as a memorial.

The objects are real; she can touch them. After all, it's the objects in fairy tales that are irresistible, catalytic. For the secrets they represent but cannot divulge. The golden ball. The blood-stained key. The enchanted teapot. The robe of feathers.

She remembers Deborah Eisenberg's "Form and Theory of Fiction" class in graduate school. Where she learned to glean from Nikolai Gogol and Felisberto Hernández and Bruno Schulz. Mansfield and Kawabata and Tanizaki. It was the first class she'd ever cried in; also the first class where she had looked up from a page spattered with her own hot tears and seen her professor crying too.

•

She walks the four streets over to the poet's house. Found sculptures line the yard: antique fans, metal conveyor belts, a typewriter with a tiny plastic figure of Ruth Bader Ginsburg. Hula-Hoops on the cactus arms. Rusting metal teapots. There are two mannequins in the poet's living room—one a sexy neon pink.

That day, the poet had received a steroid shot in her wrist and sent her a photograph from the doctor's office: a hand with what looked at first glance to be gold foil pasted across the knuckles. It turned out to only be the physician's anatomical model of a hand, its pale-yellow joints laid bare from lack of skin. But still, an object to marvel at. Like the vintage typewriters in the poet's front yard.

Now that she's begun to lose people, she feels the metaphor of the beach at the end of the world more keenly. Though that, too, may not be what it seems. We may drop our baggage at the beach and step into the sky. Only to return and pick it up again.

What is life, after all, but this kind of gleaning? What does it mean to be different in the way that Varda describes? (She thinks of the past week—the choir teacher gleaning Elgar from the tremulous vocal cords of middle schoolers, her neuroscientist friend gleaning secrets from cadavers.) To search out meaning, to pick up what's left so nothing is wasted? And that's the idea: Nothing is wasted. Not the grime, not the imperfections, not the histories, not the shadows.

To step into the morning with its first crushed-leaf scent of fall. Pick blossoms to feed the baby tortoises. Know there's a kind of luminousness with its aching past clinging to everyone she sees.

To stand in line at the bakery, the Franciscan saint balanced on the building cornice with its solemn hands, its shoulders collecting mourning doves. To walk over the Arroyo Chico bridge, carrying a warm loaf of bread in one's arms. To regard a ruby-throated hummingbird perched on a branch of velvet mesquite.

She has begun this essay thinking about patina. Thinking about her life. Now she is casting off the layers. And in the end, it isn't about her life after all.

To be a gleaner in the world: a finder and keeper of mysteries, of secret kindnesses, of things that take time to notice. The soot and weather. The colors and sheen. To choose how you want to move through the world, how you train yourself to perceive.

She places her hand on her heart for you. You gleaning birdsong, you gleaning languages. She wants to tell you a word she was taught by her Japanese friend—komorebi is "the magical atmosphere created by sunlight filtering through leaves."

Wedding of the Foxes

Every year on her birthday, or sometimes a few days after, she watches Kurosawa's *Dreams*. At some point, she usually falls asleep. That's okay, because she knows all eight short films by heart and the first two are her favorites.

When she was in grad school, as a present for her twenty-fifth birthday, a friend that had just turned the same age came out to visit her in Charlottesville. Driving to the airport, she passed sign after sign for New York City, and when her friend got in the car, her friend said, "I've been thinking: We should go to New York City," so they did. They just kept driving.

That was when the Met was showing the exhibition *Surrealism: Desire Unbound*, and she remembers feeling transported before she even entered the building, the moment she began walking up the steps. For the next two hours, she was a paper cutout threading past a dimensional world—remade into a gash, a translucent mouth, a wing.

In the gift shop, she bought *A Book of Surrealist Games*. Not seeing it anywhere else for decades afterward, it felt like a special talisman, a secret handbook. Paul Éluard's: "There is another world, and it is in this one." She believed.

She started the birthday film tradition because she wanted to do something besides hating her birthday and because it reminds her of something useful. Each of the eight short films is based on recurring dreams of Kurosawa's. He made them into a film; it wasn't an easy task. Most people dismiss their dreams—Kurosawa built a replica of his childhood home just so he could film the first vignette.

The dreams themselves were important. This is why she watches them. It's what she wants to remember.

•

She has two favorite language games from the book. One is the "Game of Conditionals." The other is the "Game of Opposites."

The "Conditionals" game is for two or more players. The "first player must write a hypothetical sentence beginning with 'If' or 'When,'" then conceal it. The second player then writes a sentence in the conditional or future tense.

The example: If there were no guillotine
                  Wasps would take off their corsets.

•

In Kurosawa's first film, *Sunshine Through the Rain*, a little boy stands in front of his house as a rainstorm begins. The sun, however, is still shining—the boy's mother warns him to stay at home because the foxes hold their wedding processions in this kind of weather and don't like to be seen.

The little boy stands under the eaves as his mother hurries inside with her bamboo umbrella. Maybe he thinks for a moment about what foxes might do if they get angry. Then he slips away into the trees.

Would you go to see the secret wedding procession of the foxes?

The game of opposites also contains a fold-over list. The "first player writes a sentence, a question or a statement, at the head of a sheet of paper, and passes it to the next player." The next player then writes exactly the opposite of that sentence, either parsing it phrase by phrase or responding in any "opposite" way to the idea. The first sentence is then concealed by folding over the paper. The list continues, alternating affirmative and negative.

She likes to play a slightly different version by translating an entire poem, line by line, into its opposite. Turning something into its opposite is an exercise of possibilities. She likes that.

When the boy returns after viewing the fox wedding from behind a tree, his mother hands him a knife. An angry fox has been looking for him, she says, his transgression so terrible that the knife was left for him to kill himself. Go quickly, his mother says, find the foxes and tell them how sorry you are. (This is a child's dream; she appreciates that the terror is authentic.)

The boy doesn't know where to go. His mother says that on days like this there are always rainbows. That foxes live under rainbows. That he must be ready to die. Then she shuts the door. And he walks to find the rainbow, holding the foxes' knife.

What's the opposite of a rainbow? What's the opposite of a knife?

There is a reason these first two films are important. In the first film, the boy, for example, could have tried to hide or run away. Maybe even woken from the dream. Instead, he sets out to find the foxes and ask for their forgiveness, though in doing so, he risks his life. The next scene shows him walking in a field of wildflowers so saturated with colorful blossoms his small figure is nearly swallowed. The flowers feel essential and hyperreal. As if the fields have adorned themselves to the limits of abandon in their efforts to encourage his apology. Impassioned, they seem to urge him on.

•

When she's invited to a residency at an ecology institute, she mentions ecologist and anthropologist Imanishi Kinji's book *The World of Living Things* in a talk. "Our intuitive knowledge of resemblances [as a species] determines our affinity towards other species," Imanishi argues, "thereby resulting in our subjective response."

Who do we as humans have an affinity for?

In her PowerPoint, she had a picture of a pug puppy next to a picture of an endangered freshwater mussel. The ecologists had nodded; they studied fog-dominated forests, algae blooms, urban insects.

The transgressions of humans toward more-than-human species have become dire. To ask forgiveness is an act of opposites. To contemplate repair over destruction; to honor diverse intelligences, weddings, and ways of being beside our own; to reject the illusion of human exceptionalism—these are acts of revolution.

•

In Kurosawa's second film, *The Peach Orchard*, a little boy follows a girl outside to the family peach orchard, which has recently been cut down. It's a spring holiday, Hinamatsuri, the Doll Festival. The elaborately costumed dolls he'd just been viewing at home appear on the stepped hillside orchard as people.

Since the holiday is for the peach blossoms, they explain to the little boy that they are "the spirits of the [peach] trees, the life of the blossoms."

The spirits of the tree taunt him, but the boy surprises them with his earnest and impassioned tears: He loved the trees, he told the spirits; he hadn't wanted his family to fell them. When the spirits mockingly presume he only desired the trees for their peaches, he protests. "No!" he cries. "Peaches can be bought. Where can you buy a whole orchard in bloom?"

This is her favorite moment of *Dreams*. Because the spirits have made assumptions and are taken aback by his sincerity. Because they'd made the mistake of dismissing him as a child, then recognized him as a person.

And because they honor his personhood with a gift: They perform a ritualized dance that allows, for a few shining moments, the peach trees and their blossoms to reappear. It moves her to think of the boy setting out to ask forgiveness from the foxes. To see the reincarnated spirits of the peach trees.

To value human and nonhuman life—life we may not have a natural affinity for. "In order to change ways of being," André Breton tells us, "we must first change ways of seeing." Perhaps that means we must dream it before we see it.

•

A year after her daughter was born, she won an award and was flown out to Los Angeles to give a reading. One morning she and her partner slipped out of the formal events and went to the LACMA exhibit on women surrealists. There were many delights. (Among them, Breton's 1920s sexism and the male gaze subverted, absented.)

But her favorite was Dorothea Tanning's self-portrait—appropriately titled "Birthday." She recognized it; she'd seen it at the Met.

It's a portrait of latent and simmering power: The woman is bare-breasted; her dress is exotic and feral—Renaissance sleeves and seaweed teeming with creatures—as if she's just strolled into the house from under the sea. Before her crouches a basilisk; behind her, an open door, which leads to a reflected infinitude of other open doors. The woman stares straight out of the painting, her gaze encapsulating surrealism's magnetism.

As she stood there in the gallery, her bra stuffed with pads so her own aching breasts wouldn't leak breast milk onto her blouse, she felt it, she couldn't turn away: Every single one of us is more than we seem.

And by "us," she means the foxes and peach trees too.

As artist Ben Denham argues, "What matters here is not just the worlds produced by scientific inquiry but also the other worlds produced by experimental practices of all kinds in which the problem—the risk, the danger, the mess—of an engagement with forces we don't fully comprehend, of our experiments not turning out as we might want, hope or imagine, is fundamental to the practice."

If there is to be a new kind of environmental revolution
We will hear the statues in all the gardens of the world
begin to weep.

The surrealists dreamed of revolution too.

•

Paul Klee says, "Art does not reproduce the visible; rather, it makes visible." She remembers this when looking at examples of her favorite visual technique, "inimage," in which "sections are cut away from an already existing image in order to create a new one."

But she also likes Hans Arp's torn-paper collage. In which fragments of cut or torn paper are tossed onto a page and glued. In moments of particularly acute existential anxiety, this is what she does.

She likes the cheap, off-white construction paper best; she buys it from the dollar store. It doesn't make as much noise when you tear it, so she can construct the collages while the kids are asleep.

For the surrealists, it was about the dreams themselves, but more—the tools that allowed them access to the marvelous, to the subconscious, to the dreaming mind. The critic Michael Richardson says: "Surrealism, then, neither aims to subvert realism, as does the fantastic, nor does it try to transcend it. It looks for different means by which to explore reality itself."

It seems important to note that "Exquisite Corpse" and other surrealist games were collaborative, collective activities.

Later, when they move to Fairfax, Virginia, she visits the Hirshhorn in DC. The exhibit: *Marvelous Objects: Surrealist Sculptures from Paris to New York.*

Some of the objects were ethereal—Dora Maar's *Untitled (Hand-Shell)*, for example—a woman's hand extending from a large seashell like a crab. And a sculpture she couldn't seem to draw herself away from: Alberto Giacometti's *No More Play*, a marble game board with enigmatic pieces whose cool arctic beauty begged to be touched. Who were the players? What was the game?

She recalls the Magritte biography: "Everything we see hides another thing; we always want to see what is hidden by what we see. There is an interest in that which is hidden and which the visible does not show us." In other words, a marvelous object is also a reverie.

Against the wall, Maurice Henry's *Homage to Paganini*, the bandaged violin set in a box of artificial grass. She was disappointed to see it in front of her; its presence and vulnerability existed so differently inside her head. Inside her head! Of course! *It lived inside her head*. What stood before her was simply a former representation.

•

Imagine this: You are dreaming. There is a knock at the door. You open it and recognize the visitor and must make a decision to either let the visitor in or close the door. Write down what you decide and why.

Play in a group. Each person is given a writing utensil and paper. Each one takes a turn to announce the name of a visitor. At the end of the game, read the results aloud.

Other categories of objects: natural objects, perturbed objects, interpreted, book, mathematical, poem-objects. Mobile and mute objects, involuntary objects, phantom objects, being objects—the list continues.

Most people don't know that Méret Oppenheim's infamous 1936 *Object*, the fur-lined teacup, saucer, and spoon, is made with gazelle fur. Today, most gazelle species are threatened. One—the Queen of Sheba's gazelle—is extinct.

Another little-known fact: The original Dalí *Aphrodisiac Telephone* was constructed with a real lobster. Dalí meant for the exhibit to have an olfactory component: The lobster would eventually putrefy, thereby transforming desire into disgust and reminding a viewer (rather viscerally) of their own mortality. But after the exhibition, Dalí's patron convinced him to make a facsimile. Eleven plaster lobsters were constructed: four that were rust-colored on a black telephone, and seven that were off-white on an off-white telephone. The goal was the displacement of the expected. The estrangement, the defamiliarization.

The idea of a living being as part of a surrealist object assemblage intrigues her. Like another of Méret Oppenheim's found objects: a bicycle seat covered with bees.

•

She begins to renew an old practice—like Oppenheim, she starts paying attention to her dreams. In October, after she'd watched Kurosawa's *Dreams*, she started dreaming about pilgrimages.

In one dream, she watched as a woman she didn't recognize dragged a life-sized wooden saint to an empty clay alcove and heaved it inside. The woman wore a brown dress, something crenulated. Fancy, but ripped on one side and streaked at the hem with mud. The woman placed her hands, exhausted, on the saint's thin, feminine shoulders. And when she turned around, a crack opened in her neck like wood. It was clogged with bees.

The pilgrimage dreams continue. Until one night, lying there, with her hand on her own bare neck, she inexplicably remembers how badly she'd wanted to see *Yayoi Kusama: Infinity Mirrors* when they'd lived in Fairfax, Virginia. Her partner had tried several times to get tickets but had never been able to.

She gets out of bed, gulps down a glass of water, and googles it. Discovers there is a Kusama installation exactly one hour and forty-eight minutes from her house. The Infinity Mirror Room titled: *You Who Are Getting Obliterated in the Dancing Swarm of Fireflies*. Then she laughs: She's been using her left hand to navigate the computer. Her right hand is still on her neck, covering the crack with the dream-bees.

In the early 2000s, Kusama began to make complex, dimly lit, mirrored rooms, a departure from earlier installations that were brightly illuminated and full of circular polka dots.

She'd been warned that Kusama's Infinity Mirror Rooms—especially the dim ones—can be tricky to navigate. One might actually run into a wall. But words can't prepare for that fundamental sense of bodily disorientation, or maybe it's cognitive as well—that slipping into someone else's mind.

On the placard outside, Kusama explains: "Become one with eternity. Obliterate your personality. Earth is only one polka dot among the million stars in the cosmos."

Our earth. Our foxes, mussels, peach trees.

•

It isn't what you might think; you have to walk through strands of lights that are suspended from the ceiling. You have to brush through them as if they're bioluminescent filaments of seaweed and you're walking underwater. Or in space.

And the photos don't show the confusion of bodies, the gasps or shuffled feet, the disoriented exclamations. But at some point, her eyes adjust, and her son's terrified grip loosens a little on her hand. They stand in the corner, inside someone else's dream, wearing their gray silhouettes, the lights buoyant, adrift around them.

They are gashes. Translucent mouths. Wings.

"What is admirable about the fantastic is that there is no longer anything fantastic: There is only the real," says Breton.

Would you go to ask forgiveness of the foxes?

Would you open the door?

Blue Horizon

TAWADA YŌKO

Dear Tawada Yōko,

There's a plastic bag on my dresser full of old brass doorknobs. I went searching for them at a place on 22nd Street, where people drop off building materials: outdated ceiling fans, extra shower tiles from their bathroom renovation, rusting medicine cabinets they've dug out of the wall so they can slather the hole with a piece of drywall to install a new, shiny mirror.

The cashier—a woman with neon purple hair tinged with silver at the roots—was fastidiously folding pairs of underwear on the glass counter (they have a section for clothing too) when I set the doorknobs down. "Well, my dear," she told me as she unwrinkled a Safeway shopping bag and placed each dull and clanking piece inside, "you're going to need some elbow grease."

I frequent that store because it's one of the only places where I can find household materials to repair our house that are from a suitable time period: the 1950s—1951, to be exact. But she's wrong about the elbow grease. I prefer their patina. Grabbing my bag and walking past the toilets and sinks that lay like discarded fossils on the asphalt outside, I had to laugh because I remembered that moment in your story—"Where Europe Begins," when the narrator is traveling by ship to a harbor town in Eastern Siberia.

"Next to the library," the narrator says, "was the dining room, which was always empty during the day. The ship rolled on the stormy seas, and the passengers stayed in bed. I stood alone in the dining room, watching plates on the tables slide back and forth without being touched. All at once I realized I'd been expecting this stormy day for years, since I was a child."

It haunted me, the thought of standing there, watching those dishes slide back and forth across the table in that empty dining room, the certainty of the feeling that one was arriving at the very moment one had been waiting for most of one's life. Because in the moment I read it, I felt that I was a person who had been waiting all these years to inhabit that moment in your story. I say inhabit on purpose—I was no longer reading it.

Those fractured fragments of a travelogue in which a lesser writer's hands would have felt abrupt become a receptacle of strange and exhilarating possibility. I had the sense of passing through the most intense of human emotions without the danger of perishing. A Fire Bird and Samoyedic fairy tales, dreams of frozen factory chickens flapping to life from the frying pan, childhood memories of eating monstrous squid, a white streamer tossed from a departing ship whose act of disintegration obliterated memory—one cannot help but emerge from the reverie with a sense that the world has been enlarged; the tiny keyhole you have been pressing your eye to and calling it "life" has surrendered its mirage and you've stepped through.

I wonder, are you also someone who feels the presence of others, even when they are not there? Someone who wonders how often a doorknob has been turned, and in whose hands and upon what threshold? Are you someone who thinks about certain lush moments you have left to live that are there in the glittering distance, just waiting for you to arrive?

I like the study of objects—dishes, doorknobs—how they can remind us of things and people that have come before us and that will come after us. They have been touched by hands, and perhaps repaired by them. They carry time in their bodies yet remain mysteriously open-ended in their interpretation. My hand passing through a long line of hands that have turned a particular doorknob; my body as one of many bodies walking through whatever space exists beyond. That fundamental sense that the tidy narratives we carry are only tidy because that's the space we've permitted them to exist in. That the truth is what falls through the cracks and blurs into other moments. That what the objects really carry—mutely, mysteriously, and even if we can only sense them—are those stories.

Like this blue horizon teapot, the one that I take out when I read your work. It's made of gray stoneware, with a brushed cerulean line that circles its silky smooth belly, and you can splay your hands on it, like on the belly of a fat cat. It's the one I took out that rainy morning after walking the kids to school with my friend AS when she asked me what we call a certain type of cloud formation—the thin, high glaze of dappled clouds—in English. Some type of cumulus, I said, maybe cirro? She said, "We call them fish-scale clouds." And in the moment that she said it, the clouds seemed to stretch out in the sky like the curved, tensile body of a fish whose refracted scale-edges glinted with drops of water slipping from some otherworldly sea.

It's a teapot I return to when my life feels like the color has been slowly leaching out: the day I'm sitting in the airless room with ES while the doctor tells her she has cancer, or the third week in a row that one of the kids has been sick and utterly miserable. It's not just the objects, but whatever makes us remember to view our own lives more expansively.

There's a fascinating essay on weathering in which ecofeminist philosophers Astrida Neimanis and Rachel Loewen Walker talk about how we must imagine our bodies in "thick time," permeated with rain and sunlight and the climate intra-actions around us—"Like all other bodies of water, human bodies are replenished by rain; the winds that whip around us also fill our lungs and feed our blood; the sun's warmth allows us, like sea algae and sunflowers, to flourish." They ask us to critically examine the "myth that human bodies are discrete in space and time, somehow outside of the natural milieu that sustains them and indeed transits through them."

It reminds me of the moment in your story "Where Europe Begins" when the narrator says, "When I was a little girl, I never believed there was such a thing as foreign water, for I had always thought of the globe as a sphere of water with all sorts of small and large islands swimming on it. Water had to be the same everywhere. Sometimes in sleep I heard the murmur of the water that flowed beneath the main island of Japan."

Sometimes I hear that murmur too. In pandemic homeschool, I taught my daughter the water cycle. The diagram of water circling through its forms: vapor, solid, liquid—each water molecule lifted from its perfumes, from its salts, from the scratches of its former life over and over. We made rain in a plastic bottle with ice and warm water, and the tips of our fingers were stained with blue sea dye for days.

Now, when I take out the blue horizon teapot, I try to listen to the water before I drink it. Where it's moved. Through root systems of ancient cypresses, the gills of snowflake moray eels. The whoosh and sluice of the grand-piano-heavy heart of a brachiosaurus, the slip down Athens's Peisistratid aqueduct. Inside water bottles carried in orange life rafts at Lesvos and shallow soda lakes radiating the cries of lesser flamingos. Through Mt. Fuji's snowmelt and South Carolina's Venus flytraps, Venetian glassmakers and Persian poets, and an ornithologist's water glass as she studies her finches.

Like watching a glass house rise inside a glass house inside a glass house until an entire glimmering city—just at the point of being made finally visible—collapses in a tidal wave of droplets that dissipate, then rise into air.

You make me remember: Even when the world is asleep, I can listen for the murmurs. Not because I think I can translate the language. I listen because it helps me remember that it's there.

With gratitude and admiration,
Katherine

Haunted Household Objects

In White Sands, New Mexico, she hikes up the dunes with her family. The sand is made of gypsum, which, unlike other desert sands, is cool to the touch. The dunes seem to trace the contours of an endless body. They exist because 280 million years ago in the Permian, this area was covered with a shallow sea.

Agnès Varda tells us: "If we opened people up, we'd find landscapes. If we opened me up, we'd find beaches." When she crouches in the dunes and sifts the silky gypsum crystals through her fingers, she thinks: If they opened me up, they'd find the Permian Sea.

That the body can be a landscape; that the body can be tied to earlier histories.

No, not just can—is.

•

In natural history museums, the Permian Sea dioramas are her favorite. Rugose corals, nautiloids, and brachiopods—"lamp shells," since their shapes resemble little clay oil lamps. It floods her body with warmth to think of it: Shallow seas would be full of sunlight after all.

Gypsum is not sand—it's a mineral that can dissolve in water. In crystal form, it's actually clear. But the wind tumbles and rasps those surfaces, scratches them opaque. Not sea-foam white or cloud white. A kind of otherworldly brightness. The kind of whiteness against which ghosts might appear.

Later that trip, they visit the Museum of International Folk Art in Santa Fe, where she finds an exhibit on yōkai: the "ghosts and demons of Japan." Shape-shifters, specters, and supernatural beings described as both "ghastly and comical." There is an eighteenth-century parade-of-monsters scroll, a fairy-tale book titled *The Tongue-Cut Sparrow*. There's an unnerving video installation of the wooden head of a smiling geisha that splits open to reveal horns and a massive set of pointed teeth.

Once home, she checks out every library book on yōkai she can find, even the graphic novels. Learns about amikiri—a lobster-shaped yōkai with enormous scissors instead of hands that likes to snip mosquito nets. A hajikkaki—a blobby, pale creature so shy it lives underground (and if you dig it up, will curse you with something shameful or embarrassing). Monster cats, women with ravenous mouths in the back of their heads, mountain goblins, mermaids with carp bodies, foxes that transform into samurai messengers—the list goes on.

But her favorite by far are the haunted household objects: tsukumogami.

•

She sometimes imagines that these places she is trying to tell you about are only accessible from dark rooms with sets of complicated staircases. You can never see the room you are trying to get to; you can only see, step by step, the stairs you need to take to arrive. In her mind, these staircases are lit by grainy spotlights—monochromatic, diffuse. In her mind, these staircases are full of sand.

•

Tsukumogami translates to "ninety-nine spirit"—referencing the idea that any object, upon reaching ninety-nine years of age, could become animate. As authors Hiroko Yoda and Matt Alt explain: "The roots of tsukumogami are found in the animistic tradition of Japan's native religion of Shintō, which holds that not only human beings but all things, living or inanimate, can be repositories for souls."

The sixteenth-century scroll *Tsukumogami Emaki* (Illustrated Scroll of Animals) is a brief tale about a collection of used household objects (a tea kettle, a bamboo shamoji or rice spoon, an old kimono, etc.) that have turned into yōkai. As Saitō Maori tells us, "Sometime in the Kōhō era (964–968), during the year's spring cleaning, a number of old utensils are ungratefully discarded. Because of their intense sense of indignation at being cast away, these disgruntled utensils become animated, bent on getting revenge on their human owners." The utensils party and rabble-rouse and cause a ruckus. And eventually, end up at the Tō-ji Temple and become enlightened.

There are hundreds of these tales from the Muromachi period. Many are accompanied by exquisite illustrations. Her favorite drawing in the *Tsukumogami Emaki* is the one-eyed rice spoon (shamoji). But she also loves the four-legged tea kettle, and the prayer bead string with its little faces.

Tsukumogami can be haunted teapots turned into tanuki—Japanese raccoon dogs. Shōji screens that fill with watchful eyes. Or paper lanterns with faces, ancient mirrors that gain sentience. There's even a grater that transforms into a porcupine.

With small children, the domestic becomes a sphere that is all-encompassing. Dishes. Bottles. Spoons. The tsukumogami interest her. It isn't a stretch to imagine the walls have eyes. That the mirror is possessed, the bed has an attitude problem. "Artifact-spirits," "haunted-relics," "thing-wraiths." At the museum, there was a giclée print of contemporary tsukumogami: a Kleenex box with legs, a couch with an open maw.

When she reads they are known to be furious if discarded after serving their human owners so faithfully, she laughs out loud. As a mother, she can relate to this.

•

When she says if they opened her up, they'd find the Permian Sea, she means it both metaphorically and literally. The end of the Permian was the world's most extreme extinction event. Our bodies are here because our bodies moved through those bodies that survived it.

Consider: If all life living now has a common ancestor, if her body has DNA in common with seahorses, lemurs, honeybees, those bodies aren't just other "animals." They're her siblings.

Ecofeminist Lisa Kemmerer tells us, "Through dualism, those living in patriarchies tend to view the world in terms of opposites, beginning with male and female, and extending to a plethora of other contrived divisions, such as white/other races, human/animal, culture/nature, and reason/emotion."

Landscape/*Body*. Human/*Nature*. Human/*Animal*: false dichotomies. The idea that we must leave the human world to cross over to the natural world is a false dichotomy. The human/nature binary is a construct of humans.

We are the natural world. We are the world's body. There is no separation.

•

Perhaps she can't help thinking about the Permian Sea these days because we find ourselves again in a place of mass extinction.

Kemmerer again: "Most ecofeminists reject dichotomies and hierarchies as alien to the natural world—nature is interconnections."

A writing friend tells her the math of this essay is loose. If a body is a landscape, can it also contain a landscape, he asks? What's up with all the haunted objects? And where do all the staircases go?

She is aware that in this essay, things are spilling into other things. She knows the math is loose. That the staircases are now pouring sand. And yet.

This essay is feeling around in the dark for pieces that have been forgotten, pieces that are missing. This essay looks at Constantin Brâncuși's *Sleeping Muse* and wonders where the rest of the body is, and why museums only ever build display cases for the disembodied heads. Maybe the muse's body, invisible, is huge. And beautifully monstrous.

Maybe her body is everywhere. Perhaps that's the reason this essay is trying to build a different kind of staircase.

•

Here's what's interesting to her about the tsukumogami. Reading about them begins to subtly change her. Washing a teacup. Cleaning a mirror. Drying a spoon. *All of these things someday could be alive*, she finds herself thinking. *Perhaps they are living now.*

That possibility: When one believes a thing is conscious, one treats it with tenderness. She knows this might sound strange. She admits it felt strange to see this happening to her too. Now, she finds herself doing things that she's never done before. For example, in Marie Kondo's infamous book on tidying, she suggests you hold an object and thank it for its service before letting it go. Here's the difference: When, following Kondo's directive, she thanks an object now, she imagines that it *hears* her.

Not adopting animism as a practice exactly. But rather, recognizing that the boundaries are blurry. That trying to continue to see things differently, to listen differently, is a practice too.

In her book, *Vibrant Matter: A Political Ecology of Things*, philosopher Jane Bennett asks us: What are the implications of considering everything as animated—including landfills, rocks, metals, and electricity? To think not in life/matter binaries, but rather to consider ourselves as participants in swarms of entangled, interconnected, jostling bodies that are constantly shifting, being modified and transformed? "For example," Bennet asks, how "would patterns of consumption change if we faced not litter, rubbish, trash, or 'the recycling,' but an accumulating pile of lively and potentially dangerous matter?"

One could argue that the current environmental crisis is a crisis of vision and vision*ing*—that is, the inability to imagine realities and trajectories other than the ones we are currently living. Also, the inability to envision what our current trajectory will end up looking like.

Which leads to this thought experiment:

Suppose there is a house, and in this house, the household objects are portals in which spirits can slip in. Let's say there's a woman that lives in this house, who, upon reading of the new extinctions—the Spix's macaw, for example—begins to think she hears the cries of birds from the powdery turquoise of her coffee cups, the pottery bowl that holds her fruit.

Let's say she ignores it for a while: The job of caretaking her two young children is both monotonous and immense. Anyone that sleep deprived is a little unhinged.

But let's say the woman in that house begins to dream of another house. A much larger house, filled with other spirits. Now her children are a little older, and she starts to notice more inexplicably odd occurrences. Her shower curtain, for example. When it gets wet, it squeaks the "chaa-chaa, chaa-chaa" call of a lime-green Réunion parakeet.

Let's say it becomes clear there are now staircases back and forth between these houses, and in her house, other spirits have started showing up in other objects—a trickle that quickly becomes a stream.

Suddenly, her teapot coos at her like a Mariana fruit dove. Her mirror, when she's washing her face, flaps its reflective surface shut with a set of monarch butterfly wings. The clock on the dining room wall blinks at her with the amber eyes of a Seychelles scops owl. Her snow leopard lamp stretches its paws at dusk, then curls up, purring in moonlight.

Let's say part of the reason this essay must come to life is because she's afraid if nothing is done to stop these particular hauntings, they will spill out from these doors and into the houses of her children and their children too.

Let's say she begins to write a book because she realizes that it never has just been about *her* house or *her* children.

This, too, is a false dichotomy.

•

Here's her point: What if we had to live, remembering? Would we do something different if we knew we'd have to live alongside ghosts?

When one believes a thing is conscious, one treats it with tenderness. Perhaps even this essay is thrumming with the desire to be more than a boundaried object. Even this essay is learning to be alive.

Her daughter likes a subspecies of tsukumogami: the "teapot samurai." It's made entirely of discarded dinnerware: the head of a sake bottle, body of a teapot, skirt of a soup bowl (inverted), and arms and legs of whatever discarded utensils happen to be lying around. Unlike Humpty Dumpty, she's warned, the seto-taishō can reassemble after a fall.

She likes this thought too. That lost and broken things don't just reanimate but can continue to self-repair.

•

There were so many more staircases than she realized. Staircases not just to rooms but to other houses, other mothers. Staircases to so many other beings. Can you hear the sand now? It's falling faster, sifting down with its *swish, swish, swish.*

If you can hear it, that's because the staircases are not staircases at all, and the houses are not houses. There is no out that is not in. It is an invention, this being separate.

Her body is the Permian Sea. Your body is the old-growth forest of Fontainebleau. This soapy dish carries the spirit of a Ganges river dolphin.

Seagulls

ŌBA MINAKO

Dear Ōba Minako,

I write this away from the desert, in the mountains in the eastern part of Arizona. I can hear my family laughing as they call forth creatures they find hidden in the knotted pine walls of the mountain cabin. "Snake wearing teeny tiny boots!" my son calls, and I imagine him fluffed like a bird in piles of blankets. "Alligator with one eyelash!" Eventually, the walls grow silent as they leave to take a walk to the creek.

The valley below is wreathed in clouds. What is it about floating places that make us feel the strangeness of our lives with clarity? Your stories are floating places, too, places often in transition: coastlines shrouded in fog, cemeteries where graves are eclipsed behind curtains of moss. They are strange stories—of mountain witches, and fringe characters dropped suddenly into foreign cultures—characters whose resilience becomes apparent only when they draw on their powers of imagination.

Watching the clouds makes me think of the quietness in your story "The Pale Fox"—the part when the narrator talks about mushrooms she sees while her father guides her through the forest to an overgrown tomb where he'd thought he'd glimpsed the ghost of her mother. "The path was slippery with mud, and fungi that reminded her of withered and broken oranges grew from the fallen tree trunks. There were others with plump, fleshy umbrellas that spread wide like patches of snow."

I don't know how many times I've read this story or how often I've considered your evocative technique of naming people after creatures (like your narrator's lovers "Pale Fox" and "Praying Mantis"). I know that I return to it because of what it makes me feel: the hush of contemplation, the hush of generative solitude.

I say solitude, but I'm not talking about being alone. I'm talking about something quite different.

Have you read Gaston Bachelard? He has a chapter in *The Poetics of Space* titled "Intimate Immensity." In it, he argues that the poetic experience of reverie has the capacity to extend beyond an individual's intimate realm and into external space with the expansive space of imagination as a place the two can enlarge one another. He uses Rilke as an example:

> ... A travers nous s'envolent
> Les oiseaux en silence. O, moi qui veux grandir
> Je regarde au dehors, et l'arbre en moi grandit.
>
> (... Silently the birds
> Fly through us. O, I, who long to grow,
> I look outside myself, and the tree inside me grows.)

As Bachelard argues, "The two kinds of space, intimate space and exterior space, keep encouraging each other, as it were, in their growth." Later, he says, "it is through their 'immensity' that these two kinds of space—the space of intimacy and world space—blend. When human solitude deepens, then the two immensities touch and become identical."

When I make tea in the stoneware seagull teapot, I think about Noriko Mizuta Lippit and Kyoko Iriye Selden writing in their introduction to your translated work, "Minako had a long period of submergence as a housewife living in the United States, completely out of touch with Japanese literary circles. During those years [...] she stored observations of life as well as her own frustration, creating a rich reservoir of imagination on which her expression, once it was released could draw heavily."

I drink my tea and think about you living for more than a decade in that remote village in Alaska. Of what you found there, and what sustained you. Of what you thought of the days you were deep-bone tired, and what you promised yourself you'd write when you could. I think about the mono no aware—"the empathy toward things, the awareness of impermanence"—that I inhabit certain moments with a kind of shattering clarity when I read your work.

This teapot is the one my son likes best. The birds are simple: blue ink sketches on a backdrop of gray. Even the heavy, circular lid is painted: gulls both at the shoreline and in the sky. I like how the scene on the teapot is a flock of the loudest birds that's utterly quiet.

As I've read your stories, I've thought more about solitudes. Like this morning, when, after being up for the last three nights with a sick kid, my brain feels half junk drawer, half cloud chamber. I can't see very well because in my nocturnal shuffling, I've snapped yet another pair of new glasses, and since I'm fairly certain the tingling I feel moving in waves across my skin is the same virus snaking through my veins, I'm not sure if I should go take a nap on my daughter's enormous stuffed penguin or just put my head down and cry from sheer frustration.

And yet—lush quiet is exactly what I'm talking about. Solitudes in which I can rest, in which my breath and being can expand instead of contract. I think that's why I started collecting the teapots. And why I read everything I could of your work. Because even in the middle of the DC suburbs, even when I couldn't get out to a wild space after driving for hours, even after I'd lie awake in the middle of the night, my exhaustion roaring inside me like a terrible wind, I could read your words and carry their expanses with me.

Like this moment in which the narrator describes how the father discovered the tomb in the first place. "It was like the abalone clinging to the rocks. Somewhere down among the forest of gently waving sea tangle there comes the glitter of a fish's belly, and suddenly you see it, the tight, tender flesh of the abalone enclosed in its shell, deep within the lush growth of moss." The story continues, "The shells of the abalone were hidden by sea moss; the tomb was covered with forest moss. When she bent to examine the moss more closely, the beauty of a microcosmic world spread out before her. The stone tomb beneath it became an illusion [. . .]." When I wrote to your translator, he told me that this part of the story was based on an experience you had when you accompanied an elderly Kawabata Yasunari searching for an abandoned grave site. That the juxtaposition of beauty and the grotesque is a recurrent theme in your work. I think that's what solitude holds as well: the wildernesses of both.

Here's another thing he wrote: "I recall Minako speaking of her experience as a young teenager during the war when she was recruited to work in a clothing depot. She said that whenever there was an air raid, all the managers and staff would go to the air raid shelter, but since there was not enough room there for the schoolgirls, they were instructed to run out into a nearby field and lie down. She said that was the best part of the day because they could take a break from work. And she also enjoyed watching the silver planes with their contrails crossing the blue sky, and when the bombs went off, they created beautiful fireworks displays. Through her imagination, she was able to transform this horrendous bombing into a beautiful fantasy."

"Immensity is within ourselves," Bachelard instructs. Ōba Minako, you taught me and I carried that immensity, and carry it still—your strange mushrooms, that little glint of abalone in the pull of all that dark water.

In these mountains, finding those kinds of lush solitudes is easier. Because the summer rains bring strange and voluptuous crops of mushrooms to the mountains, today, the children hiked with sticks. That way, they could prod the mushrooms without fear of poisoning, extract the moist, plump stems to studiously examine the way one might pry, then replace, stucco from the wall of a crumbling forest cathedral.

And the space in these mountains—with its fallen timbers, its airy thatch of leaves, its submerged veins of rose quartz that break open in the stream with glinting facets of crystal—is more than a cathedral. It's a place my solitude rises to meet it, and in which my solitude accepts its presence and becomes vaster because of it. It's a place where oranges sprout from dead trees, and where snow can shimmer even in the heat of summer.

What strikes me: That particular reverie of seeing mushrooms as broken oranges and patches of snow allows the imagination to see such creatures in a way that we were never taught to consider they existed. We may now know glimmers: That vast mycelium networks communicate between the submerged roots of trees, and that fungi are capable of sending electrical signals that have a striking structural similarity to human speech, but there is undoubtedly more that is unknown and undiscovered. Yet your imagination allows me the practice of inhabiting the strange and wonderful possibilities of their existence.

And I can say this—I reach for those fallen trees and the presences that inhabit them and touch them as if they are bodies, and as my family and I rest there, quietly leaning on those collapsing giants, our solitudes grow large enough to hold forests, and foxes, and intricate microcosms, and constellations rear up and leap through the clear vaults of our being like deer.

>With gratitude and admiration,
>Katherine

The Crane Wife

Pilgrimage

Every Valentine's Day, her family drives out to see the cranes.

They drive past signs for Western Hydro Engineering and Tim's Electric. It's windy when they finally set out on the trail, but clear. The kids pull their hoodies past their ears. Crumple their masks and shove them in their pockets.

Drifting from somewhere above them is a thin smell of burning grass.

"They leave their roost to feed at dawn," her daughter reads from the sign at the trailhead, "returning for a few hours in the late morning. Some migrate as far as Siberia to breeding grounds."

Sandhill cranes. Known by the slash of scarlet on their forehead, their seven-foot wingspan. Their elaborate courtship dance.

Dream People I

They visit her when she's asleep. Past loves. Difficult friends. Loved ones that disappeared before she could adequately say goodbye. Always because something has been broken or left unresolved, unable to be repaired.

Settings are variable but recurrent. A planetarium. A cliff on the edge of a highway where a bloody deer carcass seeps beneath a tarp. A terraced island in Uganda. A hotel room in Budapest. A bedroom filled with unopened greeting cards. A gothic house—somehow her house but falling into ruin, the greenhouse windows shattered, the laboratory benches slathered with dust.

With some, there is a longing that makes the aura of the dream spill over to her waking life, so she walks around all morning with the dream still clinging to her like sticky fog.

She calls them her Dream People. Each dream person like a weather balloon tracking some internal emotional barometer to which she has no access. They disappear and reappear like ghosts.

Birds Near and Far

A few months before the COVID-19 pandemic started, a paper was published in *Science*.

The findings: From the 1970s to the current time, about half a century, almost 30 percent of the continent's avian populations have been lost.

Birds have been disappearing. Not just vulnerable or threatened species, but backyard birds—sparrows and finches. Migrating birds, too, saw a steep decline. Five hundred and twenty-nine species were studied.

When she read the headline citing the *Science* paper in *The New York Times*, "Silent Skies: Billions of North American Birds Have Vanished," she felt the air rush into her lungs and stiffen there. As if her lungs were stones that had just been frozen.

Sandhill cranes are still relatively abundant. But of the world's fifteen crane species, ten are threatened with extinction.

Language and Erasure I

Hyginus writes in *Fabulae* that Mercury invented several letters of the Greek alphabet after watching the patterns made by cranes in flight. She likes that idea—that human language could be inspired by birds. That letters and languages can be found in the sky.

Tasting Salt

Their son refuses to wear any shoes besides flip-flops these days, and in the February chill, his feet are cold. Up the trail, she carries him on her back for a while, her hands wrapped tightly across the bare tops of his feet. When they run into a couple on their way back from the spring, they learn that the cranes aren't there; the rains haven't come, and there isn't enough water.

Because of the COVID-19 pandemic, they have to semi-shout this information across the wide dirt path.

Indeed, the ground is parched. The grasses blonde and brittle, the white mud dried and curled into little puzzle-pieces. The soil shines with a white crust; looking closely, you can see little glittering crystals. She crouches down and tastes it, thinking she probably shouldn't. It's gritty, sulfurous.

But then the kids are kicking off their shoes and tumbling down little hillocks of scrappy grass, stomping down knobs of dirt. They skid down the crushed earth, shrieking, then studiously extract little curls of mud, arrange the fragile polygons.

Impermanence has new meaning these days. She recalls reading that the oldest-known crane fossil dates to ten million years.

The Crane Wife I

She bought the book on eBay, but it came from a public library. With the little pocket to grip the checkout card. The cardstock littered with stamps. Dates that have existed but are now long past. How many different kinds of hands had turned these pages? There's a stamp in large letters on the inner pages: WITHDRAWN.

She wanted to find the same book her mother read to her when she was a child. Her son likes the page where the man finds the wounded bird in the snow. A brushstroked flurry: You can't tell if the swishes are snowflakes or feathers. Its wing is pierced by an arrow. Very gently, very carefully, the man draws out the arrow and tends to the wound.

"But Mom, how could he have heard outside?" Her son asks the question after she reads that the crane's dragging wing had made a rustling sound.

She wasn't sure. "Well," he decides, "it would either have to be very quiet, or the man would have had to be listening."

After the man removes the arrow and releases the bird, late that night there is a tapping at his door. A beautiful woman appears and begs to be his wife. He's overjoyed. Gently he takes her hand and leads her inside. But he's a poor man. So his wife tells him she will weave for him. Weave a cloth of the finest silken fabric. Of course, there's one agreement: He cannot watch her do it.

Vulnerable and Endangered Cranes I

Most crane pairs extend their wings, and leap and pirouette when performing their courtship dance. Blue cranes also run in parallel, the female taking the lead. Hooded cranes circle each other when courting, tossing grass and feathers into the air. When wintering in the Gulf of Texas, whooping cranes eat wolfberries and blue crabs. Red-crowned cranes have a patch of skin on their crown that turns bright crimson during mating season. Sarus cranes are the tallest flying bird, measuring almost six feet. When young wattled cranes are in danger, their parents shove them into tall grasses to hide. The heads of grey crowned cranes and black crowned cranes display tufts of stiff, gold-colored feathers. Siberian cranes fly more than three thousand miles during their migration and can live more than eighty years. White-naped cranes are the only cranes that have a gray-and-white striped neck and pink legs. Cranes can be found on every continent except South America and Antarctica.

Dream People II

Lake Bunyonyi, "Lake of Little Birds," is found in southern Uganda and is home to East African or grey crowned cranes. When she was a student at Makerere University in Kampala, she traveled by boat to Bwama Island in Lake Bunyonyi. It was lushly beautiful, full of green terraces thatched in places with wild blooming poinsettias. On the island, she met a group of people affected with leprosy—wards of the island church and the last members of a leprosy settlement dating back decades. They were cured, but most were blind and terribly disfigured. It was clear that at least some were still in pain. One woman—a double amputee—noticed her, and reached out to her with hands that had mere stumps for fingers. "Please," the woman said. There is no other way to say this—every last Lugandan word she'd been learning stuck like glue inside her throat, and she tried to give some money to the woman but couldn't bring herself to touch the woman's hands. The crumpled bills fell to the ground and she stood there, stupidly, helplessly, watching the woman scrabble for the money in the dirt.

Rowing back to the mainland, she felt the kind of shame that makes your body feel like it's being boiled. There had been a bird—a single East African crane—standing in the shallows, watching as her paddle dipped into the lake. From that moment on, the image of the crane and the woman became inextricably linked in her mind.

They moved the settlement from Bwama Island years ago. It is all but erased. But now that woman and the crane are some of her Dream People. They return to her. And she remembers.

The Crane Wife II

Lately, she's been thinking about the way the suffering of more-than-human bodies is erased.

The whooping cranes electrocuted by power lines in Florida. Poachers cutting off the wings of demoiselle cranes in Zhob Valley and cramming them into boxes to be sold as pets. Siberian cranes dying of pesticide exposure in the Liao River. Blue cranes found poisoned in the Overberg.

She wants to understand the structures that allow this to happen. Structures so normalized they're nearly invisible. And the stories that make these structures persist.

For example, if she was the husband in *The Crane Wife*, would she have noticed? Would she have asked? If she'd seen the wife emerge from weaving—each time paler, thinner, withdrawn?

The violence of that page when he finds her, her suffering no longer hidden. The door ajar. The crane with her head thrown back, the spattered blood smeared across her wing.

Didn't he suspect she was the crane? That she was plucking her own feathers to weave him his cloth?

After all, the fabric seemed to glow *with a light all its own*.

Dream People III

While listening to music on her iTunes playlist, there is a sudden eruption of sound. It takes her a moment to realize it's the call of an East African crane—something she'd downloaded while researching crane species. A momentary scrap of sound. A fragment of a bird call from the past. Then the music played on. What if the Dream People of our future are the extinct birds of our past?

The Crane Wife III

Last week, she opened a box of architecture drawing supplies that she found at the thrift store. She was looking for a mid-century desk lamp. Instead, she came home with a little kit of architecture stencils for the children: colored pencils, blueprints.

Inside one of the notebooks, she found a child's diligent sketches. She likes the untitled, four-tiered pagoda best—it's exquisite and cleverly rendered in lavender ink.

The pagoda makes her think of *The Crane Wife*. And how one inhabits a story. The pagoda is a story too. The way that human thought is a story.

Story #1: The couple lives in a four-tiered pagoda. The husband, once poor, now possesses a house that the neighbors whisper greedily about, has a strangely beautiful wife. But it is not enough; he's saturated with his neighbor's greed. The wife grows paler, the sunlight sluggish. His sleep grows shallow, dreamless. He discovers his wife is a crane because she kills herself trying to weave for him. Instead of grieving, he starts to hunt. Not to eat but to skin and mount the birds. Until at night, his bedroom swarms with the silhouettes of dead cranes.

Story #2: The husband has decided to place mirrors in the four-tiered pagoda so that every corner may be stunned with light. Except the husband notices that his wife would rather stand at the windows than the mirrors. That's when the cranes begin to collect on the lawn, the eaves. As if they're drawn to the house, magnetized by it. It's impossible to scrape their droppings from the graveled paths. One morning, he wakes up to find his arms are stippled with tiny barbs that later become feathers, then eventually, wings.

Story #3: The wife has died. Her body has been carried off by birds. The husband, disheveled by grief, devotes his life to building a bird sanctuary that will later welcome poets. Those poets will write poems of the future that will mostly be about species of the past. Birds like fruit doves. Snowy owls.

Story #4: The wife refuses his ridiculous request, kicks the husband out of the pagoda, reengineers the entire structure to be biophilic. Pollinator plants for butterfly migrations, berry bushes for birds, compost for the earthworms. In the winter, even in subzero temperatures, she'll trudge out of the house with two buckets to feed the red-crowned cranes.

Story #5: The plants have taken over the house, seeded the stone garden Jizō's heads with moss and rivulets of roaches. Ectotherms and humans have vanished. Slushy clouds obscure the sun. Thistles sprout improbably from the ceiling, the middle of the staircase. The only birds left are holograms.

Story #6: Do you see? It could be any story now. In which story are the red-crowned cranes, the black-necked, and Siberian cranes saved? In which story do they vanish? Stories, as philosopher-writers Thom van Dooren and Matthew Chrulew remind us, "do not just recount connectivities; they also weave new ones. They are about forging relationships, about learning to see and understand, and, as a result, about being drawn into new obligations and responsibilities."

She folds the blueprint and stuffs it back in the little box, the pagoda now a watermarked blueprint in her own mind. *Who are you that's invented this house that now inhabits me? Where are you now?*

She feels so moved by these diligent creations of an unknown young person that she can't throw the sketches away. So she takes them from the notebook and hides them in her letter drawer.

Vulnerable and   II

Most   pairs extend their wings, and
                        dance. Blue   also run in parallel,
                        . Hooded   circle each other
                                            into the air.

                        . Red-crowned   have
                                bright scarlet
Sarus   are the tallest flying   almost
When young wattled   are in danger,
                to hide.
        black crowned cranes display   gold-colored
feathers.
                                                White-naped
        are the only   that have
            pink legs. Cranes can be found on every   except

Dream People IV

She lives within walking distance of her local zoo, and some mornings, visits the southern white rhino enclosure. The space is sprawling; most people don't look past the rhino and its pool of mud. But in the corner is the feeding station for a pair of East African cranes. Every species in the enclosure—the southern white rhino, East African crane, and Speke's gazelle—is endangered.

Sometimes, we forget that a species is actually composed of individuals. These two cranes—a female and male, though not a mated pair—are named Tina Turner and Sly. Tina is in her forties and much older than Sly. Both like to boss around the Speke's gazelles. Both have crowns of golden feathers that the sign mentions are useful for hiding in tall grasses.

She likes to watch them walk. Their careful precision. The way they can bend a leg backward and balance on the other without falling. The deliberate splay of each foot when it meets the ground.

The Crane Wife IV

She doesn't mean to diminish the story in any way. She still finds it provocatively strange and alluring in its melancholy pronouncements. And she would argue—along with scholars and other lovers of the tale—that the primary emphasis is cautionary, a story meant to expose the pitfalls of human greed.

Yes, that much is clear. But she's interested in the nuances, the substories, the narratives so seamless they seem transparent. Fragments that have lodged in her and other bodies without their noticing.

For example, in the book she owns, it's fascinating that what makes the crane wife finally fly away is not that the husband asked her to do the weaving but because, as the crane wife says to him, "You looked upon me in my suffering." In other versions of the story, the crane wife leaves not because he sees her suffering, but because he finds out she's a bird.

Meaning: In *this* version, she would have stayed, even on the verge of dying, had he not looked in on her weaving the cloth? She would have stayed if she had just been able *to suffer silently?*

Which may not be the worst thing she's heard. But also may be the worst thing she's heard. The thought of any living being suffering silently is ultimately problematic too.

Inbreeding Depression

In her conservation genetics class, they studied the genetics of small populations. How deleterious recessive alleles—genes that cause deformity and reduced survival, among other difficulties—become more prevalent when populations are small. Not only can this increase extinction risk, it also means that individuals in an isolated population can become more sickly and vulnerable.

It's a devastating thought: not just the extinction of a species, but the idea that even before the last individual is lost, the final remaining individuals of that species can be diminished, made sickly, abnormal.

Dream People V

Her Dream People are quiet. That's what used to make them so terrible. They could find her anywhere. She will not lie: She used to hate how they made her feel. Impotent, helpless. But now she's no longer so afraid of them. To lose her Dream People would mean losing the resonance of memory, would be its own kind of erasure. Now, she tries to treat them with tenderness. Bringing them to the light as if they are books made of elemental things: air, and water. Tries to notice their subtle textures and strange fragilities, the different ways she is asked to leaf through their pain. Maybe there are some texts we're meant to read over and over. Maybe there are some ghosts that change us only by continuing to return.

Language and Erasure II

When writers talk about erasures, they use words like "deconstruction" and "symbolic effect." When biologists talk about erasure, they use words like "extinction risk" and "inbreeding depression." But when she thinks of erasure, she thinks in smaller, more subtle units. Those fragile interactions and shifts in the relationship between human and more-than-human species that will no longer exist. No small pause to notice a butterfly passing. Languages being wiped from the sky. Here's the problem with extinction: It can happen so quietly that one doesn't notice. Species suffer silently then disappear.

              and   III

Most   extend   , and

                                              circle

                  the air.

                                                flying

almost

        to hide.

                feathers.

                        the only

                              except

.

Language and Erasure III

She likes that word "except." It makes her think of what poet Srikanth Reddy says about poetic erasures. That "there are countless texts hidden within any text," that "when you erase a text, you're 'unearthing' possibilities of phrasing, voicing, and thinking that are already embedded but somehow buried or hidden within the language."

    So, one can think about the silence of a space in which cranes disappear, their suffering invisible. And one can think about a space in which the text can be shifted. A space in which whooping cranes have been brought back from the edge of extinction, rural farmers have fed red-crowned cranes during harsh Hokkaidō winters, and the flyways of Siberian cranes are protected.

It makes her remember a story she'd been told in Uganda: One hot summer day, a chief had gotten lost while hunting. Dying of thirst, he asked several animals—an elephant, a zebra, and a gazelle for water. Because he'd hunted them, they refused to help. Then, a flock of cranes flew by. When he asked, they'd brought him water and led him home.

To reward the cranes, he gifted each of them a crown made of gold. But they came to see him without their golden crowns the following day, complaining that the other animals had jealously stolen and destroyed them. So the chief called his court magician. Where the magician touched each crane on the head, a crown of golden feathers grew.

Cranes IV

Most

                                                         cranes circle

                                            flying

                      in

crowns of   gold

                    and can live more

                                        be found

Ponds

She and her family drive to a different location. Out to effluent ponds next to a golf course, which is really not a golf course unless you can imagine a driving range chiseled out of a mealy swath of sand.

And there they find them.

Hundreds of sandhill cranes clumped in groups just inside the pond. Their gray plumage reflected in the pond's dark mirror, their necks and wings stretching and collapsing like curls of smoke.

Broken Toy Party

Today, she played "broken toy party" with her son and his dinosaurs. Each dinosaur brings her son a toy that's broken, and he fixes it. The toys are little blocks that he likes to build with. The dilophosaurus has broken his surfboard. The pink triceratops's hedgehog has lost his stuffing. Each toy gets fixed, and then the dinosaurs gather around him and thank him, and it makes his whole face light up like someone's just switched on something inside him.

In his memoir, Tanizaki recalls his grandfather's lamp-lighting business. This was during the Meiji era, in shitamachi. The lamplighters—many of them former samurai down on their luck—would set out with their ladders. They'd climb up, open a little glass window, and light the oil. She can imagine them fanning out over the streets with serious expressions. They wore uniforms: tight-fitting pants and coats adorned with burning suns. What that must have looked like. Then, as now, light was a serious business.

"What does light eat?" her son asks in the car. They're late to her daughter's swimming practice; she's only half listening because this question comes after a barrage of other questions about what trees eat and stop signs eat, etc., etc. Also, she's starving. "Shadows," she says without thinking of it. And only later does it occur to her how untrue that is. Or is it?

Francis Ponge has been called the "poet of things" for poems that lyrically examine single objects—an orange, an oyster, a door, a pebble—in such a way that the object is made utterly new. She loves the opening line of Ponge's "The Candle": *Night sometimes revives a curious plant whose light decomposes furnished rooms into clumps of shadows.* How he captures the animate strangeness of an inanimate object's life, its atmospheric ability to dismantle a room.

She gets the text at 7:49 on a Tuesday morning, ten months into the COVID-19 pandemic. *Can you stand in witness tonight at about 5:30 for L., two houses down from mine? Her mom died yesterday, her brother a few days ago. Just stand for a few minutes and leave our candles.* She writes back: *Of course.*

The neighbor who texts her has recently also lost her mother as well as her beloved dog. She is the neighbor who has left on her front porch steps, in no particular order, a vase of snap pea shoots for the baby desert tortoises, a roll of gingerbread dough for the kids to make cookies, a bag of still-warm garden zucchini. In certain exhausting moments of the pandemic, she recalls a conversation they'd had about depression. Here's what you do about it, her neighbor tells her. Every night you're grateful for three things. You have to really contemplate them and then write them down. And every day, you do three thoughtful things for other people.

She and her children glue scraps of colored tissue paper onto glass jam jars, then light candles and drop them in. The part that moves her most is how walking down the street, other neighbors join them. After being sequestered in their houses so long, the procession feels like something happening outside of time. When they arrive, each person moves forward to set a candle down. It's an eclectic display: tall votive candles, candles in hand-thrown clay holders, little flames simmering through bright lozenges of tissue paper.

Ponge often took two to three years to write a single object poem. Stole half an hour each day from work (and sleep) to write. She feels that what he's captured about the candle is essential: There's a kind of light whose tender care of dark places induces their shattering.

The vigils continue. Another time, this text: *Candlelight vigil for A., the wonderful dog companion of J. & J. who left our world today.* Sometimes there is a photograph. Sometimes, the person speaks. *Thank you for coming. It's been a difficult day.* If so moved, others share memories. Sometimes, not many words are spoken. Just, *It's so beautiful to see you all here.* Then tears.

A single candle is a wisp, a nearly imperceptible glitch. But more, together—sanctuary.

Sometimes, the dinosaurs go to the pool. They use painter's tape to stick blocks together. Fill the opening with glass gems used for wedding vases. When you run your fingers through this "water," the gems clink with soothing music; they are cool to the touch. The armored dinosaurs make the biggest splashes, and the other dinosaurs cheer them on. In the desert, water, too, is a place of refuge.

From Ponge: *Its golden leaf, held by a very black peduncle [. . .] encourages the reader to go on.*

After reading this, she begins to think of candles not as objects but as gold-leafed companions.

One night, she's called to a neighbor's house. Even as she turns the corner, she can see the unearthly flicker of the fire trucks' lights. When the fireman tells the group that it will likely be many hours before EM's body can be removed from the house, that the police have to complete their investigation, and confirm her cause of death was COVID-19, the neighbors wordlessly disperse and return a few minutes later with chairs. The fireman is moved by the communal gesture and, for a moment, turns away, shading his face with his hand. Fresh grief is a profound and agonizing intimacy. Hours collect in increments: stuttering lights, the hard glint of uniform regalia, bats whirling in the dark.

"If light is scarce," Tanizaki says, "then light is scarce; we will immerse ourselves in the darkness and there discover its own particular beauty." JW lights white votive candles and places them on the stone pillars that surround the front yard so it's lit when the mortuary transport car arrives. You know this, no one has to tell you. Candlelight is fundamentally a different kind of light.

After this night, she starts lighting candles for dinner. Tall ones that the children fight over who will blow out first. Tea lights in Swedish candle holders made of frosted glass. It seems to work best when the days grow shorter, when the light outside the tall windows dims. *Glow,* she thinks. *Illumination.* From the Latin *illuminationem,* "to throw into light."

But it's not just the grieving; it's the commitment to participating in it together. It bears mentioning that at the broken toy party all the dinosaurs are required to attend.

Mt. Fuji

ŌTA YŌKO

Dear Ōta Yōko,

The first time I read your story "Residues of Squalor," I couldn't stop thinking about the slugs. That opening scene—June rains drenching a set of shabby dwellings in Hiroshima, hastily assembled in the aftermath of the atomic bomb—and the way the narrator describes the slugs infesting the crumbling buildings, breeding and multiplying beneath the floors. How she watches their forms creeping up the aged, green mosquito nets under which her relatives lie sleeping, "their molluscan bodies slowly undulating." It's a detail too repulsive to feel invented.

So many of the story's details were too harrowing to feel invented. And even before I discovered that you had survived the bombing, I couldn't help but feel your ghost slipping in and out of your characters. You know what I mean. When you sense the resonance of lived experience subtly scaffolding the woven walls of fiction. After I read your biography, each moment began to carry a new weight. To think of a city built on corpses. Birds bursting into flame midair. A memoir scrawled on wastepaper and shōji paper screens. Neighbors constantly preparing for the funerals of children.

It's strange; each time I work on this letter, it's as if I can feel your presence. Like you're standing over my shoulder, quietly contemplating the page. Maybe it's just because it's the middle of the night again and I'm listening to the squeak-scritch of the bitter orange tree's branches against the window glass. Thinking about the reasons I turn to your work when reality seems unbearable. Maybe it's time to set the pen down and make us a cup of tea. I don't mind having tea with ghosts, especially if the ghost is you.

•

I said the first time I read the story, I couldn't stop thinking about the slugs. And who wouldn't for the way they function so symbolically—sticky remnants of uncontainable horror, a miasma of faceless, rubbery bodies whose infestation seems to signify an endless welling up of calamity, ruin, despair.

But as I reread it, I noticed things I hadn't before. First, the story did not, as I had recalled, actually begin with the slugs. Second, what it does begin with is something subtle, but quite profound. The narrator says, "At midnight, when the world was hushed in sleep, this awful-looking hovel did not stand alone in solitude, for around it hundreds of identical houses stood side by side, and human beings were alive, asleep in those houses. When I thought of this, my mind was, unusually, at peace. [. . .] I felt as though the warm breath of those asleep reached my skin from neighboring houses not one iota different from the one in which I was sitting."

It's a serene thought: the insomniac surrounded by the warm collective breath of sleeping forms around her, their presence bringing her consolation. Even on that soggy parade ground built on top of corpses. Even with the radiation sickness already coursing through their blood.

•

This past summer I sat in a car with my friend as he talked to me about being molested as a child by his piano teacher. And I told him about what it was like to have my sanity shredded by postpartum depression; to feel as exhausted and distant as a dead star, unable to eat or sleep.

When I think of your narrator—awake in the soundless dark watching slugs, but also being comforted by the thought of the presence of others sharing her situation—it makes me think of that moment. And remember the solace of shared vulnerability.

Vulnerability. It's not an easy word, nor is it an easy emotion to experience. Its Latin root, *vulnus*, quite literally translates as "wound." But it's in the knowing and sharing of wounds that care and connection are made possible. I read about the bitter criticism your writing received in Tokyo. Critics who scrutinized how the work displayed the "mess" of your personal life or intimated that you were trying to sensationalize your experience to revitalize your writing career. How eventually the weight of their criticism made you stop writing.

•

The teapot that's on my desk is one I don't take out very often. Its handle is cracked; the spout chipped. It's a murky gray color hand-painted with gold; out of the mist, the shape of Mt. Fuji rises in a triangular suffusion of fuchsia. The mountain is the only color the teapot has. It's the teapot I take out in unbearable moments—the sudden death, the bitter news of a dear friend's divorce, the abyss of anxiety about a child's diagnosis. Sometimes, one needs a quiet place inside the ruins.

The mountain is what I can lift my eyes to in the midst of the despair or uncertainty or grief. Not because it allows me to alter or transform the outcome. But because it reminds me that disequilibrium and chaos and brokenness are also a part of human wholeness. And that I am never alone in my despair. Not really. Even half the world away, even this very moment, someone is gazing at Mt. Fuji with a broken heart too.

•

Your narrator's life—she's intentionally left unnamed—is transparent. She's haunted by the memories of molten bodies, by the ruins of a broken love affair, by the child she has given up, and addicted to sleeping pills and narcotics she takes to numb the trauma and pain. She does not hide from us. She contemplates suicide yet does not choose it. But it's not just the observance of her struggles that makes her presence so moving.

It's when the narrator tells us that she's distressed because she doesn't want to kill the slugs the way her mother and sister do, picking them up with disposable wooden chopsticks and dropping them in a can of salt water. Peering into the can, she describes them: "They were half melting but not completely melted. Thick and muddy, there was no sign of their having put up resistance to this sole primitive measure. After once eyeing this sight, I had begun to suffer from an association about human beings heaped up in a mound of death, half-burnt but not completely melted, with no energy to show any sign of resistance. They were so alike. I could not think of slugs as mere slugs." Repulsed by the slugs but equally queasy at these associations, she says, "I wanted somehow to save their lives."

Empathy is a response of vulnerability—to empathize cannot help but make her relive her own pain but is at the same time something that gives that pain coherence. If she is able, even after experiencing unspeakable trauma, to recognize the effect her choices have on other lives (even quietly nonhuman lives), if she chooses to feel instead of being blind to the silent suffering of the beings around her, she shows us that patterns of violence and indifference can be broken or replaced. Not through anger or disgust. Or displacement or hatred. But through curiosity, through paying attention when another being is in distress.

We are so afraid of pain. But you remind me that our most uncomfortable stories, our most painfully jagged and indissoluble griefs are also the cracked places where our luminous awareness and belonging can arrive. As in this poem by mid-Heian poet Izumi Shikibu:

> *Although the wind*
> *blows terribly here,*
> *the moonlight also leaks*
> *between the roof planks*
> *of this ruined house.*

Within the terrible wind that wakes us from sleep, inside the cracked rooms of ruin—thank you for being the moonlight.

With gratitude and admiration,
Katherine

Monarchs

ART OF GRIEVING

for Homero Gómez González and Raúl Hernández Romero

She'd ignored the sharp pain in her jaw for months, and when she finally went to the dentist, she discovered her tooth had abscessed at the root. This required a particular kind of standing X-ray that scanned her entire head. When the dentist tilted the screen to show her, she was surprised to see, peering back at her through the ghostly scrim of the screen, her own grinning skull. "No other option," her dentist said. "We'll have to extract the whole thing." It was the season of the wolf-face sulphur butterflies. She'd noticed their pale-yellow wings pasted on the sidewalks of her daughter's school.

She lives in a city located only sixty miles from the US-Mexico border. In a neighborhood where the local grocery carries fresh guavas, prickly pear pads, and apple empanadas. And, in December, tejocotes and tamarind pods to make Ponche Navideño for Christmas. Where her children's favorite summer treat is to visit Peñas Snowcones, Tacos Y Mas and order raspados made with shaved ice and fresh syrups of crushed mango, raspberry, or lime. Where you cannot stop at stoplights without noticing the candles and sun-worn silk flowers of roadside memorials. Where when her family is sick, they are gifted homemade tamales and pozole by friends. Where houses and public spaces carry ofrendas for

Día de los Muertos, and she's seen truck beds stacked high with marigolds in the last days of October. Where friends have gifted her objects to make her own.

When her younger brother first became a physician, he would call her when one of his patients died. Some awful stories. The young father that had a heart attack while swimming with his children in a hotel pool. The children were too little to pull him out; he slid from their hands to the pool bottom. Or the larger-bodied woman who died in his arms when, just after his shift, he'd walked out to the parking lot and saw her collapsed half out of her car. The young man's suicide after he'd only had one appointment and had told her brother afterward that, for the first time in a long time, he felt more hopeful. Her brother had lived in Albuquerque for his residency. At the apartment where they'd filmed the scene in *Breaking Bad* where Jane dies choking on her own vomit, and Walt stands there watching her die and does nothing. Fans of the show would sometimes collect outside his house, and when he'd leave for work, ask if they could see inside. Which, of course, he'd say no to, but then tell her on the phone—what do they want to do with that? I mean, what is it they're looking for?

Certain things are hidden inside other things. Fruit, for example, hidden inside blossoms. Butterflies hidden inside chrysalises. A speck of grit hidden inside a raindrop. All of the colors of the spectrum hidden inside white light. During pandemic homeschool, she teaches her daughter how to find the rainbow hidden inside sunlight. It turns out all you need is a glass of water, a slit in a notecard, and a window where the sun can shine through.

The eerie floating image of her skull reminded her of being a fetus and a corpse at the same time. She remembers the profiled, hazy sonograms of her children's skulls and the macabre mustiness of innumerable and unidentifiable skulls in the Paris Catacombs. Bones make language fall away like skin. At the dentist's office, her skull stared back at her as if it recognized her. That hidden thing swarming out of the screen into the glare of the overhead lights. As if surprised to have been found.

When her brother lived in Mexico, he was invited by friends to Oaxaca for Día de los Muertos. He said that he followed the paths of marigold petals all night into houses. That in candlelight the petals shone like embers. Total strangers opened their doors and told him about their loved ones, allowed him in.

Some things hide inside other things and you do not see them. For example, this morning, she walked her son to school across a wash clotted with debris swept down from the summer monsoons, and the river bottom smelled like old granite boulders and crushed creosote, and the whole time she was saying hello to other kids and parents and holding her son's hand she also held the death of her friend inside of her. The shape of her grief like a gray paper doll that, if you reached for it, would unfold and unfold its tissue-paper creases in an almost infinite progression. As she walks by the other mothers, she thinks about the paper dolls they're carrying too. How if they drew them out of their bodies, they would begin to billow like shadowy sails. What they would catch on, how they might get tangled up with each other. How they might tear.

Her grandmother was Swedish, and her grandfather Norwegian. Some of her ancestors are buried far away in a small church cemetery in Farsund, Norway. She has never been there. She does not have a single recipe of her grandmother's, though her grandmother loved to cook. In Sweden, on All Saints' Day, candles and flowers are placed on the graves of loved ones. In Norway, candles are lit by graves on Christmas Eve, where the light is sometimes scattered inside the falling snow. No one in her family ever followed these rituals. What her children know is her friend Lilly's pozole, cups of Mexican hot chocolate when the days grow cold. She grates thick cakes of chocolate on a cheese grater, then whisks it with milk and cinnamon. A little chili powder. When her family makes Swedish vaniljkakor cookies at Christmas, they make them from a recipe she found online.

She is thinking about those things hidden inside other things because she sometimes carries the deaths that her brother has carried. She can't stop thinking, for example, about the father drowned at the bottom of the pool. Or how hidden inside the holiday Día de los Muertos is the three-thousand-year-old Aztec celebration that honored both the changing seasons and the dead. (The Aztec goddess Mictēcacihuātl, "Lady of the Dead," was said to guard the bones in the underworld and oversee the festivities; her skull face often has its jaws open—she swallows the stars so that they become hidden during the day.) Another hidden thing: stars in daylight. And her name, Larson, which hides another name. Her ancestral name, Larsen, was changed on Ellis Island.

In the desert, the shift of seasons is subtle. There are no showy curtains of chlorophyll dying and leaving maples wrapped in shades of pink and scarlet (except in certain canyons high in the mountains). You mostly know it's fall by the slow change in light. How the mornings fall across the doors with a low, slanting coolness. How the lizards begin to disappear. How the Santa Rita prickly pear suffuses a deeper shade of purple.

Monarch butterflies are particularly associated with Día de los Muertos. To the Purépecha and Mazahua peoples of Mexico, monarch butterflies represent the souls of their ancestors returning to visit them. When temperatures begin to fall, millions of butterflies travel through flyway corridors across the United States, winding downward until they arrive at butterfly sanctuaries in Michoacán. Some land in her city, in her own yard, and the yards of her neighbors. Some travel more than three thousand miles.

Time rushes through our bodies; time becomes embedded in them too. What occurs to her: It's not about the tissue-paper shapes at all. It's what's behind the paper, what's been scabbed over, what the paper covers. The shapes are just what's in front of the absence. Grief (a noun) is different than grieving (a verb). Grief lives in us like weather, unpredictable and intense. If grief is a room that our bodies must carry, what place can we set it in order to grieve?

When scientists studied monarch metamorphosis, they found that caterpillars remembered the taste of certain foods when they were adult butterflies. Which seems miraculous since metamorphosis involves a nearly complete dissolving of the body—the caterpillar must digest itself before sleeping cells switch on to rapidly grow the new body parts it will need. She doesn't know what to think of this. Does it mean that some things stay inside us forever? Or that sometimes it's possible to remember things when the veils between the worlds grow thin?

She likes the thought of veils growing thin. That kind of permeability. That metamorphosis means there can be a time to live with ghosts. There can be a time to remember. That the remembering doesn't have to be a time of weighing down. It can also be filled with buoyancy.

She reads the monarchs are officially endangered. Their winter grounds are being deforested. Pesticides are systematically destroying the plants they need to survive. It suddenly brings back a memory of going mothing with one of her entomology professors. How he set out poisoned bucket traps, and the next morning, combed through hundreds of dead moths for a few rare specimens for his collection. The waste of it. The rage she felt at someone who she thought, of all people, should have known better.

Because of the pandemic, she's spent two years living with a hole in her mouth where her abscessed tooth had been. Her tongue lived with the absence of it. There was a window in the X-ray of her skull. And for more than a few days after the new tooth was placed, she still felt it—that space of the new covering the former place of absence. The dentist's assistant takes another X-ray, and for the second time, it's like looking at her own death face-to-face. But this time, she feels it tenderly. Día de los Muertos is coming; Trader Joe's is already carrying its pots of marigolds. The most beautiful part of the ritual is that the day is both grieving and celebration. The skulls are not macabre; they're colorful, jolly, full of remembrance, full of life.

Thom van Dooren tells us, "Mourning is about dwelling with a loss and so coming to appreciate what it means, how the world has changed, and how we must *ourselves* change and renew our relationships if we are to move forward from here. In this context, genuine mourning should open us into an awareness of our dependence on and relationships with those countless others being driven over the edge of extinction." In her city, thousands travel to be a part of the November All Souls Procession. Meant to honor and grieve loss. Here's the thing—the signs and pictures they hold are not just for people. Endangered species are honored too.

In Alison Hawthorne Deming's *Monarchs: A Poem Sequence*, a woman boats through a haze of monarchs, abandoning the instructions of her delicately-tuned instruments to "[steer] / instead by butterflies [. . .]."

When she hears about the murders of the monarch stewards in Michoacán, she feels the news travel across the skin of her chest in waves of chills, as if she's been struck with a virus. Homero Gómez González had first been a logger, then became an activist. His body was found floating in a well near El Rosario monarch butterfly sanctuary, a place he'd spent decades of his life working to protect. Raúl Hernández Romero's body was discovered in the Monarch Butterfly Biosphere Reserve where he'd been a butterfly tour guide. His relatives said he'd been receiving death threats from a cartel that wanted him to stop protesting the illegal logging that threatened the monarch sanctuary.

How does one live with ghosts? When she tries to learn something about Norwegian funeral traditions, she keeps reading about Norwegians' love of candles. Lighting candles not just indoors, but in the snowy cemeteries. Inside sculptures they make out of snow.

Then a friend sends her an article about grieving for glaciers. How a funeral was organized for Okjökull, the first glacier in Iceland to be declared dead. More glacial funerals followed: for the Swiss Pizol and Basòdino glaciers, the Oregon Clark glacier, and the Mexican Ayoloco glacier. The inscription on the brass plaque that commemorated Okjökull's disappearance read, "Ok is the first Icelandic glacier to lose its status as a glacier. In the next 200 years all our glaciers are expected to follow the same path. This monument is to acknowledge that we know what is happening and what needs to be done. Only you know if we did it."

What interests her is learning more restorative ways to grieve. To recognize loss yet affirm connectivity and life. When she walks through the street next to the cemetery in Nogales with her friend, there is an air of festivity—crowds of people and pan de muerto and mariachis, pastel wreaths and marigolds. And then beyond, among the gravestones, shadowy figures clustered around pockets of candlelight. On one hillside, someone playing a guitar and singing. And the soft darkness is so tangible that she simply stands there, allowing hot currents of unmappable emotion to flood through her like a summer monsoon into a hidden canyon pool.

When she takes out the box that holds the objects for her All Souls' Day shrine, she unwraps the tissue paper with care. Sets out photos of her grandparents, beloved friends. Candles, a small bowl for salt, a cup for water. A skeletal bride and groom grinning from the blue glittery recesses of a shadowbox. This time she places dead monarch butterflies on the altar that she's collected on her morning walks. Tucks a notecard beneath them. For Raúl, she writes next to one butterfly. For Homero, another. One must sometimes create a space in which to grieve.

When they find the dead baby desert tortoise while walking to the grocery store, the children do not care that it is desiccated and shriveled. They want to pick it up and take it home to bury it. She convinces them to wait until they're back from the store and they can at least put it in a bag. But on the walk home, they forget exactly which street it is, and they walk up and down trying to find it until she gets frustrated in the summer morning heat and tells them they need to go home. At the last moment, they spot it. And when they're burying it, her son says, "It's important for everyone to say something." When it's his turn, he says to the little mound with solemnity and tenderness: "I hope your afterlife has the smell of fresh trees."

During the pandemic, she and her children had seen a single milkweed plant in a neighbor's yard covered with monarch caterpillars. A little island. She calls the plant nursery to ask about the different types of milkweed her area's monarchs prefer. Goes to pick up the plants and spills dirt all over her clothes and all over her car. But then laughs because it's sort of appropriate: What's hidden inside grief—within the terrifying rupture, the undoing and unmaking—is transformation. Which, as the monarchs know, is a process that's often a riotous mess.

In the wash that morning, as she walks back from the school, she sees a cloud of brush-footed butterflies rise from the shrubs. They are brown butterflies with a small coral-colored slash on the wing. She stops for a moment to watch them and remembers the butterfly stewards. It no longer bothers her to think of the possibility of ghosts. Neurological disturbance or spectral visitation—at the bottom of every explicable thing there seems to be something unexpected and almost always inexplicable. She knows, for example, that there's a kind of light in memory. And that memory light contains something hidden too.

Her brother has now cared for so many bodies. Ushering them into life and into what is beyond. (She remembers him telling her once, during birth, a woman hemorrhaged and the blood splashed over the surgical table in waves.) What his body carries: the lives and deaths of his patients. What her body carries: his stories. Things bleeding into other things.

She thinks about the wintering forests of monarch butterflies in Mexico. Sleeping in the oyamel fir trees in clusters so dense the trees look furry. When the air warms, the butterflies awaken, pour into the air in tumbling waves. To grieve means to draw out from our bodies the folded tissue-paper shapes of our losses (tenderly, so tenderly!), until we can feel the truths they carried. To grieve is to recognize the past cannot be unmade. To grieve is to be both marked by loss and transformed by it. It is a response that takes the broken pieces and joins them so that their breakage is evident, a part of their history and wholeness.

On All Souls' Day, she stays up after everyone has gone to bed. In that space of waiting. In that pause between. She lights the candles and starts talking to her loved ones. She remembers walking through the candlelit cemetery in Nogales and listening to the laughter and singing even as the branches snapped beneath her feet like bones.

When she dies, she wants her ashes to be scattered in the Vermillion Sea. Though lately she's realized the importance of having places to return to in order to grieve. She reads about "tree burials" where cremated ashes are placed in the ground and trees are planted over them. But it turns out that feeding your ashes directly to trees is complicated. The ashes are too alkaline; without preparation, they'll likely kill it. She remembers a German commercial in which the body is feasted on by mushrooms and turned into soil. How the woman at the end of the commercial takes a handful of that loam and lets it sift through her fingers. All that soil, all those carbon atoms, tumbling again through the world—to grieve is to be moved by life, to not lived anesthetized.

Wherever her skull's atoms will eventually reside, she knows this: It turns out light can be hidden everywhere. Even inside snow.

Phoenix

TAEKO KŌNO

Dear Taeko Kōno,

I've just returned from a trip to Mexico with my family and am thinking about your short story "Crabs." I'd like to see the crabs your narrator Yūko tries so hard to find for her little nephew Takeshi—the ones with red claws she's told you can keep as pets. At the beach—our first trip back in more than two years—the hermit crabs we found were *Clibanarius digueti*. They call them blue-eyed spotted hermit crabs, but they're tiny, barely just a couple of centimeters, and unlike Yūko's, you can't take them home without killing them.

    The COVID-19 pandemic has finally receded, and the kids (one hopes) will now be able to stay in school. We've just said our goodbyes to my sister and her family; the beach towels are churning in the washing machine, the planet spins toward our star at its usual tilted angle. But nothing feels right. Exhaustion slushes through my bones like liquid metal. My nervous system has been on full alert for so long its emergency signals are like a house with faulty wiring, lights and alarms stuttering on and off with no recognizable pattern. At night, when I look up at the night sky, the layered atmosphere feels fragile. The constellations wobble.

    Times when I feel deeply unwell, it's the sea I crave. The Vermillion Sea we've just returned from that is a four-hour drive across the US-Mexico border. Wave sounds to grind down the gritty edges of my insomnia, a tendrilled creature to watch unfurl in a tide pool. So each time your narrator insists that time alone at the sea would allow her to finally regain her health after her long struggle with tuberculosis, I can feel my own body tense with longing.

When her husband finally relents and leaves her to convalesce at the Soto-Bōshū seaside, she describes how "her lethargy, the heaviness in her shoulders, the depressions and vexations of heart which for so long had been entrenched in her body had melted away in an instant. With each passing day, she felt her body grow stronger." I can nearly smell the brine and sunshine in those pages. See the waves coil and curl around the shellfish and tattered seaweeds in the hollows of the rocks. When she describes what it means to arrive in that place, a tiny, hidden latch springs open in my rib cage, and a silken current of air surges into my lungs. Words on a page, words on a page. Yet I find that I, too, am able to breathe again.

•

Just two nights ago, I went walking with my son, who is the same age as Takeshi. I stopped midstep when I smelled the blossoms of orange trees—saturated, invisible, a heady perfume. This morning I awoke, and the entirety of our little backyard orchard is in bloom. And the lemon tree is full of tiny lavender-colored buds that I'm certain will break into blossom in the next few days. Spring has arrived. But I'm not thinking about spring. I'm thinking about winter.

What does it mean to choose—as Yūko did—rest and slowness? To stop rushing around and take a little while to retreat, to go dormant? To withdraw from the mad rush of human news—new mass shootings, new atrocities—and engage with time and the business of being in an altogether different way?

It was winter when these same trees were stripped bare of leaves, fruit, and flowers. But they were far from dead. Their metabolic processes and growth had slowed; they drew on the stored starch in their roots for sustenance. A certain number of hours of dormancy at these winter temperatures—named chill hours or vernalization—are required to regulate growth. Without them, flowers may not blossom, or the tree might set bloom irregularly. But it isn't just trees that pause. The tortoises were hibernating in the burrows. The spadefoot toads were sleeping underground.

•

I have a fifty-year-old Eiraku ware teapot—gold painted over a rust-colored background. I've often seen these teapots embellished with dragons, but mine is hand-painted with the dragon's complement, the phoenix. I couldn't help but feel the teapot was meant to find me; it reminded me of what I most desired at the time: rest and transformation, and both seemed difficult and fraught to achieve. I wanted to break free from the weight of the pandemic with some kind of new insight or transcendence, but before I did, I wanted to let the whole dislocating time be consumed, along with its bitterly divisive and dehumanizing rhetoric. I wanted to sink into dormancy, gather myself before trying to emerge again.

But it's the Greek phoenix that is reborn from the ashes. The Japanese hōō—a phoenix-like creature that is the one found on my teapot—is a divine, pure spirit that supposedly appears only in the most peaceful and auspicious of places. It doesn't die and become reborn. Its arrival is rare and often marks the beginning of a new era (while its disappearance indicates disharmony and unrest).

This was somehow a truer thing to discover: There hasn't been a cathartic end to the pandemic, or other forms of trauma endured during this period. And I'd felt anything but transformed or transcendent. But I did feel the need for enchantment. For the presence of the divine in the midst of the ordinary. What I hadn't realized until recently was just how close it was.

•

About a year ago, I discovered that the traditional Japanese calendar is not composed, as the Western one is, of four distinct seasons. Instead, it contains seventy-two microseasons, each marking seasonal variations and subtle transitions in the natural world. The twenty-four main divisions, sekki, are split again into three kō, with each kō lasting about five days. I wonder—is this the calendar that you followed?

I love how the titles of the microseasons are beautifully provocative, noting the time when "frogs start singing" or "rainbows hide." Because there were so many things I couldn't do—travel, visit loved ones—I tried to pay attention instead to the small things I could. On long walks and bike rides, I began to notice and take notes on each five-day microseason in my own landscape. Instead of bamboo shoots sprouting, I watched saguaros set crowns of white blossoms. Instead of blooming peonies, I noticed when hummingbirds began to build their nests in the arms of palo verde trees. I titled each microessay first with the kō of the Japanese calendar that corresponded to the same Gregorian date, then wrote a second title marking variations I had noticed.

What became overwhelmingly clear to me as I began to pay attention, was just how much I'd been missing. How did I not know that the mating calls of great horned owls often began in January in the middle of the night? How many nights did I stand there, barefoot, staring up into the dark stories of the eucalyptus, straining to see their forms? Why hadn't I noticed before the purple whorls in dirt that were the night-petal collections of leafcutter ants? Or the fairy dusters, whose sudden eruptions of blossoms looked like fragile rays of pink starlight?

Whole species appearing and disappearing, weaving webs and nests and chrysalises. Retreating and awakening, calling to each other with longing or warning. Young things everywhere, heaving their forms into conversation with the rest of the world. There were intimate seasons and cycles all around me, even in the midst of the city.

I learned first to notice them, then discovered them—their habits and Latin names, their preferences. The blurry backdrop of what I'd always felt was fragmented urban desert suddenly leapt into sharper focus. Intimacy engendered care: I filled feeders for the hummingbirds. Planted milkweed for the monarchs. In the skin-searing days of summer, I watered the pomegranates and eucalyptus. And they, in turn, set twilight alight with their hidden perfumes, made me stop midstep to watch the featherwink glint of iridescence at a hummingbird's throat, or the sleek rainbow streaking the side of a zebra-tailed lizard.

It wasn't just rest that I needed. My blunted senses needed to be awakened. I needed to feel the whispers of connection that reminded me I was woven into the lives of those other lives around me. Can I say it aloud—did we turn toward each other? Or was it mostly me that changed? I'm not sure. But I do know that none of that would have been possible if I hadn't stopped to pay attention. The etymology of enchantment contains the Latin word *cantare*—to sing. So many creatures had been singing, but I hadn't been able to stop long enough to hear their songs.

•

When we visited Mexico on this trip, I also took my family to El Pinacate and Gran Desierto de Altar Biosphere Reserve, a place I used to frequent when I lived at the field station. It's been recently listed as a UNESCO World Heritage Site and is notable for its dramatic dunes and volcanic past. The landscape is dotted with cinder cones, powdery black-pumice soil, and enormous craters.

There's a window of time in spring when the wildflowers sprout improbably through the thick crust of black cinders, and the entire stark landscape is carpeted with blossoms. The ones I like best are *Nama demissum*—purplemat—that translates from the Spanish as "purple carpets." The transformation from the desolate to electric purple is so extreme that one almost has to stand there, wind whistling in the ears, to comprehend it. A few weeks before or after and one misses it.

If I had to recall times in my life when I felt like I've stood in the presence of divinity, this would be among them. But I don't know how much I would have let that moment ripple through me, how much I would have been able to allow its resonance to reach me—a wing of light brushing its electricity along the dark corridors of my body—had I not been practicing a different kind of seeing and listening all year long.

•

We spent time at the estuary on this trip too. And my son found two dead sea turtles. One with the fishing line still wrapped around its neck and body. I would mention the species, but in the end, it doesn't matter. Nearly all are threatened or endangered, several critically so. And I can't help but think of what it means to pause when contemplating the magnitude of this sixth extinction and how to engender practices of repair.

It occurs to me that so many things are possible when one pauses. Space to rest. Space to imagine or reimagine. To be enchanted. To be awakened. Or simply to see clearly what was in front of you all along.

I think about Yūko advocating so fiercely to her husband that she needed to pause. Not to escape but settle into her own body. To listen to it again. By the time the story ended, I understood that it wasn't just rest she needed, but the space to reevaluate and renew her life.

•

The dominant theory of the moon's formation is one of impact: An ancient planet collided with our planet, and the resulting ejected debris field accreted to form the moon. Before this impact, the earth didn't have the tilt that gives us seasons, and days would have been much faster—some simulations show a day lasting two to three hours. Impact can alter irrevocably. But change contains possibilities. What appears at first glance catastrophic might become something different entirely—the glow of moonrise, the first snowfall on Mt. Fuji, the ebb and flow of tides.

Something reaches us, something newly born and something old as starlight. When I go outside to pick the old lemons so the new blossoms can take hold, I can feel the sun's warmth sink into the middle of my palm. It's an exchange—of light, of energy—of some unnameable thing reaching to grasp my hand through time. Can you feel it? Its heat will vanish just like the underglow edging that cloud—you have to stop, stop here, right here, right now, and feel it.

With gratitude and admiration,
Katherine

Microseasons

SELECTIONS

East Wind Melts the Ice / Owls Descend

They had been coming for a while, but she only heard them when she was awake at night, their velvet syllables floating back and forth between the Aleppo pines that towered sixty feet from the ground. She'd leave a flashlight by the door so she could slip out and look for them.

"The reason owls are nearly silent in flight," her ornithologist friend had explained, "is because the edges of their feathers can dishevel sound waves." He was right; roosting or flying, her flashlight never found them.

Until one night, like casual visitors stopping in for a cocktail, they appeared on the telephone pole in the alley just behind the backyard. Two great horned owls. If poems were birds, she thought, this is what they'd look like having a conversation. Where silence is a part of what sounds.

Suddenly she feels afraid that maybe she won't hear them anymore, that perhaps their sudden appearance means they will be moving on. That she will be alone with her whirring thoughts instead of barefoot in the neighborhood at three o'clock in the morning, breathing hard, trying to find them.

Hibernating Insects Surface / Echoes in Nesting Season

The children find a nest on their walk that has fallen from the branches of a mesquite tree.

The doorbell, which has been improperly wired, keeps ringing when no one is there.

First Peach Blossom / Wildflowers Emerge

Her favorite list essay in Sei Shōnagon's *Pillow Book* is the one titled "Things That Make One's Heart Beat Faster." Even though it was written over a thousand years ago, she finds the list moving and relatable. "To notice that one's elegant Chinese mirror has become a little cloudy," Shōnagon writes. "Sparrows feeding their young."

She thinks of this list when she notices one evening that the wildflowers have returned with their riotous colors. Seeds kicking open after sleeping all this time inside the earth. The shuddering golds of Mexican poppies, the fragile pinks of desert evening primrose. What makes her heart beat faster is thinking of the ticking of their tiny, hidden clocks—all around her, invisible bells tolling: *wake up, unfurl, regrow*. She steps with care among them, those pigment-stained petals, those hundreds of living cathedrals.

Sparrows Start to Nest / Citrus Starts to Bloom

The children decide to make their own perfume by crushing citrus blossoms in the mortar. Waxy purples in the lemon. Ivories in the grapefruit and tangerine. They mix their potions carefully, then jam them into tiny vials with small cork stoppers. Eugenio Montale knew: Lemons are vials of memory light.

The air is so heavy with scent, she wants to put it on a plate and eat it. Slice its thick perfume apart with a fork and knife like a dense piece of cake. She knows, months from now, cardboard boxes will appear on the neighborhood's walkways. Filled with fruit to be given away.

Then the air will be clear. The citrus heavy in the hand as doorknobs.

Distant Thunder / Cloudless Sulphur Butterflies Appear

She was sixteen years old at the time. Living in another country whose tropics landed much closer to the equator. She'd never seen a volcano erupt before.

Night was best for the viewing. But the mosquitoes in the marshes along the rivers were so thick she nearly inhaled them; they feasted on everyone. Even if you rubbed the bites carefully instead of scratching, they'd bleed.

It was worth it to watch the sky light up in a color that can only be described as molten neon. To see, in all that darkness, rock being born. Now, when she sees the first cloudless sulphur butterfly appear, she thinks of the same kind of light, remembering. What it means to be a witness to another's life, another new configuration arriving.

First Rainbows / Lizards Return

The lawn gnomes were strange companions. She preferred the gardens in the middle of their street, the ones with the giant Peruvian apple cactus and fairy duster shrubs and agaves that sprawled beneath the mesquites like languid octopuses.

But this yard had a kind of magic to it: There were glass balls filled with little colored fairy lights, a *Paz* sign with the word written in three different languages, ceramic fairy houses—one made from a tiny cactus instead of a mushroom. Gnomes all over.

She hadn't noticed until this year the lizards returning. Now she sees this is a yard in which they delight. Ornate tree lizards basking on the little patios. Hidden sandy nooks with greater earless lizards peeking out, a likely spot to lay their eggs. Clearly, the setup, arranged with such careful attention, had its own enchantment. Who was she to know what the lizards wanted? Who was she to know what they might enjoy?

Worms Surface / Green Oranges Fall

The clouds while driving the kids home from school: diaphanous blooms with trailing tentacles like a row of sky jellyfish. Leafing through Izumi Shikibu's poems so many times that day she'd given herself two paper cuts. She can't stop thinking about the invisible stains Shikibu mentions: the stain of a lover's body, the stain of the wind. Here, the stain is the heavy smell of green things sunning themselves. Pungent. Exuberant. All the green baby oranges rolling around on the sidewalk like someone has abandoned a game of marbles. Their scent stains the tips of her fingers.

> *Nothing*
> *in the world*
> *is usual today.*
> *This is*
> *the first morning.*

Izumi Shikibu wrote more than a thousand years ago. When she looks at the orange tree, she sees a being so full of its own bounty that it simply must let some of it go.

Silkworms Start Feasting on Mulberry Leaves /
Night-blooming Cereus Blossoms

She notices early one morning the night-blooming cereus in her neighbor's yard is full of dozens of wilting blossoms. Cereus are pollinated by hawk moths and only bloom at night—the blossoms look like feather dusters dipped in wax. Even the shredded memory of their fragrance is enough to make her kick off her bedsheets while still half asleep to find them.

What she finds instead are birds. Near the early morning, as soon as she opens the door, thousands of migrating songbirds. Warblers, flycatchers, hummingbirds. Hidden inside the newly leafed branches. Strange to see the world so still, yet hear it transformed by sound.

The following night, she steps out with her flashlight and finds a single mockingbird singing its heart out, its song brash against the stillness, and utterly singular: a sound of glass being struck, an old shower knob being squinched open over and over. A song as if some winged being has been caught in a net and is struggling, pleading for its life.

Why such anguish at midnight? She learns that young male mockingbirds grow desperate if they haven't found a mate during breeding season, sometimes singing all night in a last-ditch attempt to attract one. She knows only the human words. But is it strange to feel a kind of kinship with that loneliness? To stand there in the dark and feel her body blushing in the heat of all that longing?

Praying Mantises Hatch / Eucalyptus Sheds Its Bark

The eucalyptus has burst from its bark and its husk curls from its trunk in haphazard shreds like enormous cardboard puzzle pieces. Inside the bark, the new wood is the biting texture of alert velvet.

Her kitchen sink is overflowing with dishes. Laundry is piled in heaps on the bed. But right now, she's thinking about the way they celebrated Tsukimi—the autumn moon-viewing festival—with her friend's family by climbing up into the eucalyptus's treehouse. Eating the round, pale dumplings and watching the paper balloon moon rise in the midst of scent-heavy branches. *How do different beings experience moonlight?* She wonders, leans the length of her body against the new shining wood, this shinbone of a giant.

Irises Bloom / Stick Insects Hatch

Neon floats tossed into the pool, one fuchsia, one tangerine. The pool water pristine, the detritus of yesterday's monsoon storm—pine needles, citrus leaves—chewed away by the industrious pool sucker. When she sees the baby walking stick insect fall in, she scoops it in her hands, the little scribbly legs make her flinch. Phasmatodea, derived from the Ancient Greek φάσμα meaning "phantom" for the way they slip into the realm of the botanical yet remain animals. And who doesn't love that kind of secret? Those pieces of the world that slide so easily between one thing and another?

Despite the evocative name, a walking stick is not exactly a charismatic creature. And yet, there was a kind of fascination as the children paddled over and they watched it preen off water at the pool's edge. How it took its time, stretching its limbs one by one to slick off the offensive droplets. Carefully, tenderly, each limb seemingly the diameter of a single human hair. Three sets of eyes on a leggy insect, fingers clamped on the pool edge. It was so very hot they had to squint in the sparkle of the pool's water against the ledge where it perched, looking, well, more or less like a baby stick, and they all laughed when the last drops scattered—how it had preened its face like a cat.

Warm Winds Blow / Grackles Chatter

Great-tailed grackles tucked inside the twenty-foot hedges that skirt the wash. Their rusty-gate-hinge calls are deafening. Foliage so thick you can't see the birds—it's as if the bushes themselves are speaking.

It's scorching, so she walks before sunrise. Waters the baby mesquite trees at the poet's house because the poet is traveling. When she moves the hose, she sees an excerpt of a poem the poet has chalked across the garage.

> *Under the corpulent*
> *clouds*
>
> *I feed the birds*
> *of my failures,*
>
> *so tenderly!*
>
> —Erika L. Sánchez

The rainbow that afternoon is enormous.

Great Rains Sometimes Fall / Desert Tortoises Migrate

In the midscorch of summer, the tortoises emerge from their burrows and begin to forage. Lost tortoises are everywhere.

Her daughter finds one in their front yard, and three different people come to their house thinking it might be theirs. It isn't, but one of the three—hoping someone will do the same for their lost tortoise—adopts it anyway.

Cool Winds Blow / Figeater Beetles Swarm

It's monsoon season, air thick with moisture, sterile thunder thumping in the distance but not yet loosening its rain. Scattered in the fine dirt around the prickly pear cactus, the green iridescent bodies of figeater beetles. Among them, little mutilated cradles of hollowed-out prickly pear fruit.

They mate in throngs, lay eggs, and perish. The baby grubs winding their sleep around the dry haze of rattling leaves, around the death scrabbles of their parents, those heavy emeralds thudding the dust.

How strange and how familiar to happen upon beginnings and endings in a single space. Fecundity and death meeting like old friends in a summer house where, arm in arm, they quietly walk about, admiring the furniture.

Evening Cicadas Sing / Pieridae Butterflies Appear

Through the grime of her windshield, she watches a single yellow butterfly swerve across all four lanes of traffic. Holds her breath.

"All creatures are already dead when they live," she reads in an essay she stumbles upon while researching the heaviness of Abe Kōbō's language, his wary observations of sand and insects. "Some creatures like butterflies," Abe writes, "are more dead than others." Is that what captivates her? To be near another body that is so close to the end yet not in pain?

They'd arrived in a gust that past week, but only, she noticed, in citrus shades—fluttering lemons and buoyant tangerines. A shudder of confetti tasting the world with its feet. That their lives would be released was inevitable. The way her son only fell asleep when holding her hair.

Heat Starts to Die Down / Canyon Tree Frogs Emerge

Here's a story she remembers from her childhood: A samurai takes a brief nap beneath an ancient cedar and dreams his way into another world: Welcomed into a lush palatial estate, he's soon invited to wed the August Princess, who bears him seven children. Twenty-four idyllic years pass, his wife falls gravely ill and dies; he's told by royal messenger he is to be sent back home and wakes to find himself still beneath the cedar only moments after he'd fallen asleep.

Yet when he looks around, he finds a colony of ants, their intricate structures of straw and clay oddly familiar. Why, there is the palace, he exclaims, begins to search across the tree root for the mountain of Hanryōkō, the grave of his dead princess. Finds, embedded in clay and tucked beneath a pebble shaped like a Buddhist monument—the body of a dead female ant.

When the canyon tree frogs emerge, it's that story she thinks of as she watches the schoolchildren handle them so carelessly. Some no larger than her smallest fingernail. Don't you know? she thinks. That one is a great poet, the other has just joined the opera, the one by the bike path is a student of the moon's.

Dew Glistens White on Grass / Black Widows Start to Nest

That September, she learns that after the monsoons black widows proliferate. She finds the first one in her mailbox—feels the strands of sticky web, hears it rip as she pulls out her hand. The spider is the glassy black of chilled lava. Climbs toward her so nimbly she shrieks.

Two days later, she finds one on the backyard fence post, another beneath the seat of her daughter's bike. After that, three spherical, papery egg sacs, suspended like fingernail-sized Noguchi lamps on the gate at her daughter's school. She collects them with a stick and crushes them underfoot.

But once home, she remembers the first story she ever read of Tanizaki's. About the woman who gets the spider tattooed across her skin. She digs out the book and reads it again. "Little by little the tattoo marks began to take on the form of a huge black widow spider and by the time the night sky was paling into dawn this weird, malevolent creature had stretched its eight legs to embrace the whole of the girl's back." The woman—a timid geisha—is transformed when the tattoo is complete. Triumphant, dazzling, deadly, her "old fears have been swept away."

When does otherness turn to wonder? How is a story a door? That she begins to think of them as sisters feels salacious, a juicy secret. That she starts to delight in finding their untidy, disheveled "tangle webs." Did you know? Black widows have thousands of slit sensilla embedded in their exoskeletons; each helps the spider sense vibrations, changes shape to tune the frequencies that echo in her web.

Swallows Leave / Summer Evening Nocturnes Begin

She loves her friend's poem, where she bikes to the 7-Eleven at sunset because sometimes, when the clouds part, she can catch a glimpse of Mt. Fuji.

That morning, her son stood in front of the science museum, a human sundial. In the evening, Mexican free-tailed bats appeared in the blank sky above the park, dozens of them swooping and diving, snapping through clouds of insects that arrived with the rains.

Native fireflies in Arizona are elusive, so all afternoon she and her son had drawn fireflies on glow-in-the-dark paper and pasted them on the wall next to his bed. She'd fallen asleep reading to him. Then woke in darkness to their glow.

Insects Hole Up Underground / Leafcutters Feasting

The title of the five-day kō makes her walk outside to the part of the yard where she knows she'll find the desert leafcutters. Their underground nests can have hundreds of chambers—nurseries, garbage compartments, fungus gardens.

In the hotter months, their trails are invisible. Leafcutter ants forage in the quiet of night when the soil is cool. But the rain sage has bloomed, and now she traces the petals to their nests. It means something to see their trails loop and collide with one another, to stand still enough that she becomes implicated in their paths. She watches stragglers with their flowers held aloft like sails.

Between the prickly pear and century plant, she finds one entrance. Smeared with blossoms, a lavender corona spilled into the dirt.

Rainbows Hide / Frost Appears

The museum docent has a cross section of a saguaro cactus—he holds it up to the children to show them the saguaro's ribs. "From an early age," he says, "Tohono O'odham teach our children that they must not throw rocks or harm the saguaro when harvesting their fruit. Saguaros," he explains, "are people."

She's driven through the Sonoran Desert to the field station in the early morning when frost still lines the desert plants. She remembers how when the sun rose, each saguaro was etched in silver. They ached alive.

Deer Shed Antlers / Small Night Rains Begin

The small rain falls over her insomnia hours. She keeps her face up but closes her eyes; it treads the roof like young javelina. Her daughter had foot surgery months ago; the bone graft they used has finally begun to heal. That day she received a letter from the donor's mother: The fragment of bone they'd used in the surgery had been a section of wristbone from her son. Her son, the letter had told her, who loved to run, went into sudden cardiac arrest and died in front of his mother before reaching the floor.

Her daughter was at the pool when she opened the envelope. She sat very still at first, holding it between her fingers. Then something inside her grew white-hot and she put her forehead against the table. She wouldn't call what she did then crying. It felt like sound was being torn out of her, the way one would tear pages from a book.

The patterning of rain is eventually folded into her sleep, and when she wakes and steps out into the morning with its smell of damp creosote and slaked earth, the sense memories of dozens of desert-rain mornings crowd inside of her. Each is grafted to the next, each belongs as much as the other. Now when she rubs her daughter's foot with ointment, she thinks about that other mother, that other son.

Springs Thaw / Wind Breaks Branches

Here's what the wind has smeared: acacia pollen, the feathers of a Gila woodpecker, the carmine fruit of the prickly pear.

Here's what the wind has broken: the branch of the hundred-year-old palo verde tree, the mourning dove nest.

What has she learned? The world is speaking, all the time, that much she is certain of. What she hadn't considered, what she knows now with equal certainty, is that the world is listening to her too.

Ice Thickens on Streams / Snowflakes Drift

Snow in the desert is a dream, a mirage. The children stop everything, run barefoot out into the yard, hands up, spinning. Leaping among aloes.

There is no defter feather. It melts momentarily. Falls so quietly it reminds her of Bashō. "Real poetry is to lead a beautiful life. To live poetry is better than to write it." All begins to blur. Snow falling into abandoned nests. Snow falling like the trees require a blanket.

The doves, stunned by these chilled feathers, retreat. She sees their black eyes inside the branches, prescient, unblinking. Memory is a palimpsest, didn't you know?

What is out there is the whole world. Being erased. Reborn.

Sea Creatures

TSUSHIMA YŪKO

Dear Tsushima Yūko,

Here's what I've learned from buying a historic house. That Marrettes are the bright plastic cones that twist electrical wires together in a ceiling light fixture. That rotting wood fascia must be removed by crowbar one agonizing layer at a time. That parging is the name for the slurry you have to mix up to patch your crumbling foundation. That it's satisfying to stand on a ladder wearing my father's tool belt and use a putty knife to smooth a splintered wood corner with wood filler.

    What's occurred to me lately is how the external mirrors the internal. I am repairing our house, one project often cascading into the next in the kind of unraveling my partner now warns me about: "Don't do it, don't tug the thread." Because the entire sweater might, and often does, follow. And while I'm doing this work, I'm also writing a book about practices of repair—environmental and personal—that do not eschew messiness or imperfection or, let's be utterly honest, intense measures of frustration and regret and grief. For our damaged planet in this age of more-than-human Anthropocene, and for myself, after the years of the transformation of motherhood (territories so tricky to map) for which there are no YouTube videos I can watch like I watch the ones about restoring old brass hinges with steel wool and Brasso, or how to set pavers neatly inside a gravel path.

Autofiction is what we call it these days—fiction that's heavily invested in the author's life experience. But I like how once, in an interview, you bristled when someone suggested your work was shishōsetsu—the earlier nomenclature for the "I novel" or "confessional" form of fiction. You said this: "I write fiction, but I experience the fiction I write. In that sense, they are not fiction anymore, but reality."

Here's what's most striking to me: Certain literary themes—a divorced single mother navigating oppressive patriarchal social structures, a father's suicide and a beloved brother's death, the death of one's young son—were also the circumstances of your life, and these presences haunt your novels. Unthinkable losses. Losses that would seem to confirm the stark reality of a desolate and voracious unknown. You said, "For me, a writer is someone who has a certain biographical experience from which they draw elements with a universal dimension so as to get beyond the limits of their own experience." For you, literature was inseparable from life. You didn't want to escape from it; you wanted to go deeper in. I can't tell you how much I admire that. It's more than courage because you not only went into the darkness, you brought something back for us.

As in your story "That One Glimmering Point of Light," which seizes me with its abrupt and unsettling examination of repressed grief, one that I cannot help but read and hear the echo of the real-life loss of your eight-year-old son in an inexplicable, accidental bathtub drowning.

It is not a tidy story, nor is it easy to explain. But it maps with its own accuracy the unmooring times of grief, of a mind confronting a monstrous loss. There is a lurid and disquieting scene of a public stabbing, a mother's desperate plea for clarity in the murkiness of her own memory, an unsettling of chronological time. Loss spills through the gaps, speaks through them with its own amnesia. One could describe its subject matter as oppressive and desolate. And yet—there are moments of such radiant lucidity they have made me hold my breath each time I read them.

Like this one: "For a long while," the narrator tells us, "I had wanted to see in person, with my own eyes, the wild squirrels darting through the skies in a nighttime forest. [...] Since I knew only life in the city, the thought of squirrels gliding through the air seemed almost mystical to me." The narrator had especially wanted to take her son to see them since he was a child fascinated by the natural world: by "loaches and goldfish of every type, green caterpillars, spiders, earthworms, water beetles, water scorpions, and other aquatic creatures, along with frogs and newts, lizards and snakes."

The squirrels of the story, because they live only in the hollows of older trees and much of the nearby land has been deforested, inhabit the centuries-old trees near a Shintō shrine. In the dark, the eyes of the squirrels shine: "A person couldn't help but be captivated by the almost dazzling glimmer." But later that night, while her daughter and son can see the squirrels begin to leap from tree to tree, flying, she cannot.

It's an unexpectedly disconcerting moment, one in which the narrator's disorientation echoes her personal loss. "I didn't have a clue to what my eyes should be following. I couldn't see a thing. [...] Today, four years later, I'm having an equally difficult time locating my son. I feel like he's standing beside me. But he's not. This must be him, I think, but there is just something lacking. Even though it would be perfectly natural for him to be at my side, it is only the feeling that he is there, and I cannot draw him into my arms."

When can life become art? And art life? I've come to a point in my life where literature isn't theoretical. It isn't a game of cleverness or fluidity with language, or even making something unflinchingly radiant and able to persist after I'm gone. It's about confronting the monstrosity of being a conscious creature in a universe of too many constantly shifting threads. It's about the loneliness of being stuck in one's subjective experience, and coming to terms with the idea that we can never truly inhabit the experiences of the ones we most cherish. It's about watching those around us suffer and being powerless to help. And about the shades and nuances of deciding to continually be open to emotion and connection and vulnerability after being deeply wounded. It's about being surprised—over and over again—by beauty. It's about being lost. And found. And lost again.

Like writing this letter, which cannot reach beyond your death. And thinking that, despite this fact, I can't help but feel that there's still meaning in writing to you. And in placing your words on the page, bringing them in as many ways as I can to other readers in order to honor their presence and brilliance.

When my postpartum depression was at its worst, I used to walk out from the postage-stamp backyard of our Fairfax townhouse to a picnic table encircled by trees. I'd walk a slow loop from tree to tree, putting my hand on each one and trying hard not to look like a crazy person. I imagined them as guardians. It was a time when I'd started having the disorienting experience of depersonalization episodes—when I felt as though I were standing outside my body, watching myself exist. At my daughter's kindergarten pickup, while teaching a seminar, filling up at a gas station. Observing myself as if at any moment, I could simply turn away from my body and thus step out of my life. When I was with the trees, I was able to remember to be in my body. To hear my own heartbeat. To smell their tangle of sap and sunlight. And feel the gentle fur of their leaves.

When I read your work, I have the sense that the natural world was a grounding place for you as well. I love this moment, later in the story: "One year, we went to look at some greenhouses, nearly a dozen of which, large and small ones, had been built on a slope in a place famous for its hot springs. [. . .] The children raced ahead on their own, and I lost sight of them. Entranced on the one hand by the beautiful glass rooms—one for cactus, another for gorgon plants and water lilies, another for ferns, yet another for bougainvilleas—that enticed you one after another into a dreamlike trance; on the other hand I was stricken with anxiety and wandered around in search of my children. Just as though I still continue to wander from one glass house to another, I continue to torment myself in my dreams, dragging somewhere along behind me a sensation of sweetness as I try to locate the figure of my son."

    I still have nightmares of my son in the NICU—the alarms blaring when he would go too long without taking a breath. After the first week, my hands were so raw from the minutes of scrubbing with antiseptic soaps my knuckles bled. In my dreams, he was held not in an incubator, but in a tiny glass terrarium, and when I'd go to reach for him, my thick, clumsy fingers would be unable to handle him carefully enough, and his small body would fall apart in my hands. I recall with clarity the stories of the women around me, and the soundscape of emergency. But I know I'll never be able to write my experience into art with the kind of luminousness that you do. The kind that makes a total stranger place your books under her pillow just so she can touch them at night when she wakes.

    There's a moment in one of your interviews when you say, "I have never written about happy women. That is not because I like unhappiness, but it comes from my firm belief that misfortune is not always bad. Happiness can spoil people. Happy people can lose sensitivity [. . .]. On the contrary, people can become rich by unhappiness. Unhappy people are given a chance to discover true human nature."

    Today, I discovered that the disgusting smell in my car was a pile of rotting strawberries one of the kids had stashed in their cupholder, and it's also the day that almost every single external window of my house is painted a different color in my efforts to replace the powder-blue trim of our casement windows with something marginally of this century. Yesterday was the day we learned that ES doesn't have much time left.

But today, too, my son came home with a Venus flytrap, and in his excitement, I remembered my own excitement trying to feed my Venus flytrap when I was his age. And because your narrator wrote about her son loving carnivorous plants (and I wonder, perhaps your own son too?), it seemed only natural that I would take out the Banko ware teapot—the teapot I've come to feel is yours—while I finished writing this letter to you. It's my oldest teapot and the only one I haven't found by gleaning. This one was a birthday present to myself.

The teapot is a mash-up of sea creatures, beautifully complex. Each form shifts into another—lobster to flounder, stingray to half of a crab. A long fin becomes the underbelly of an eel, the antennae of a lobster the loop to which the handle is attached. It's a document of life's intricacy but also its inability to extricate one creature from the other. Your greenhouses, but in the form of sea creatures. Sea creatures that may—some scientists say if our current trajectory continues—have a 90 percent extinction rate by 2100.

Judith Butler says that "loss has made a tenuous 'we' of us all." But I don't think it's only loss that connects us. But what comes inside and after loss, times of intense repair or transformation—what one might call unmappable territories. Those wildernesses and wild spaces where I find myself most drawn to in order to learn how to be and see in a different way.

In your stories and novels, the presence of other lives—often nonhuman—are a kind of sustaining force. The flying squirrels, the mazes of greenhouses filled with evocative plants, the small bright presences of living things (a frog, a peculiar insect)—become touchstones of a story built ostensibly in the shifting sands of a grieving mind. Images that represent the embodied actual of the natural world.

Your writing made me remember to go in search of beauty wilds even in the places I felt most lost and ill-equipped to understand anything. Not beauty wilds in a superficial, aesthetic way. But as a practice of searching for, and being attentive to, places of encounter—however small or mundane. Of allowing instability to coexist alongside moments of pure being, remaining open even within the discomfort of the incomprehensible.

If you were sitting with me now, I'd pour some tea for you and tell you about the time I took a trip to a bay in Mexico with a group of divers. It was a strange and lonely time in my life—I'd recently broken off an engagement and had decided to go on the trip to distract myself a little by snorkeling. But when the boat sailed far past the shallows and everyone slipped inside the waves, I panicked. *You're being ridiculous*, I told myself. *Just stay by the boat*. But the water was dark and the swells were rising and then something was wrong with the ladder. I decided to just swim back to shore.

I'd always been a good swimmer, but the water was freezing, and its currents were stronger than I'd thought. My mind unhelpfully played a film on repeat of shark jaws hanging on the wall at the field station. I swam until I skirted a clearer, shallower reef and tried to calm my breathing by focusing on what I saw underwater. When the porcupinefish came into view, I thought at first it was some plastic toy ball or discarded fishing float. But it was curious about me; it swam closer.

How does one describe it? How it bobbed there in the darkness, like a sphere of smoke or fog, its fins a wispy, translucent flutter. And its skin: a kind of tensile pewter that wrinkled and unwrinkled around its eyes and spines like silk. While it had been looking at me, a piece of debris prodded past and it puffed up, inflated like a spiny, golden orb.

There are domains of emotion in which language collapses. When one is plunged into the ravishing wildness of a world that remains beyond our comprehension.

When I take out the Banko ware teapot now, it's because I want to remember. How sometimes when one body reaches toward another body, the space between them isn't space.

It was the eyes that startled me most. Like your squirrels', the porcupinefish's eyes were full of glitter.

With gratitude and admiration,
Katherine

Soap

ART OF FAILURE

SITTING ON HER DESK IS A BLACK NOTEBOOK FILLED WITH photographs of decaying buildings in Havana, Cuba, extinct parrots housed behind glass in museum specimen collections, and architectural designs for amphibious houses (houses that can float when floods occur). Beneath that book—but in direct reference to it—is a sheaf of papers that is a novel.

It is a novel about two people falling in love in front of a pile of broken pianos. About what it might mean to have the sky swept clean of birds and the ocean cleared of fish and have to create them again holographically from archived footage and specimen collections. It is a book meant to make people feel the loss of the natural world—and the weight of our current species extinction crisis—partly by understanding it through the loss and longing of a human relationship. It is a book that begins with two epigraphs:

> *Forgetting extermination is part of extermination.*
> —Jean Baudrillard, *Simulacra and Simulation*
>
> *Ua iloa i va'a lelea. / One family.*
> —Samoan proverb

It is a book she spent eight years writing in the scraps of time she had between teaching and changing diapers and reading ten thousand iterations of *Lyle, Lyle, Crocodile*. After finishing and sending it to close friends and a celebrated New York author and editor, she receives the very painful feedback that the book is, in fact, a failure.

•

The etymology of the word *failure* tells us this: from the Old French *falir*, "come to an end; err, make a mistake; let down, disappoint." But here's what's interesting: If you look back further, you see the word shares a root with Middle Persian *škarwidan*, "to stumble, stagger," and the Greek *sphallein*, "to bring or throw down." How different those meanings are. Failure: to end. And failure: to stumble.

•

Failure: to stumble is why she wants you to consider for a moment the work of poet Francis Ponge.

Ponge is perhaps best known for his poems of things—poems such as "The Candle" or "The Oyster"—in which, under his exquisite gaze, familiar objects are disheveled in the light of imagination and seen in entirely new ways. She loves the strange and alluring anthropomorphism in these poems (trees are frantic to speak, an orange is bitterly aware of its juicing). And often recalls Ponge when encountering these objects—when turning, for example, an old crystal doorknob (see Ponge's "The Pleasures of the Door").

But of his books, it's Ponge's *Soap* she turns to when she feels most demoralized, most lost. Because Ponge's *Soap* is not just a document of soap. It is also a map of failures.

•

Ponge's *Soap* "dossier," as he called it, took more than twenty-three years to complete. It's a slim volume with a guileless title. It's not a book you'd toss in your bag to read while splayed out on the pebbled beaches of the Côte d'Azur, French 75 in hand. Nevertheless, it's a book she would think to look for if she woke up to find her house on fire.

Why, of all subjects, soap, one might ask? Ponge began writing *Soap* while working for the French Resistance and continued to work on it off and on during the war. He says, "It was because we were, *then*, cruelly, unthinkably, absurdly deprived of soap (as we were, at the same time, of several essential things: bread, coal, potatoes), that I loved it, appreciated it, savoured it as though posthumously in my memory, and hoped to recreate it in poetry." Soap was that object that floated in his psyche. Soap was a symbol.

Earlier, she mentioned *Soap* is a map of failures. In fact, it maps its failures as artifact: In *Soap*, Ponge compiles drafts of the same passages that he has tried over and over to write, often mentioning where he is in space and time while he attempts—yet again—to set down the work he envisions *Soap* to be. Yet *Soap* continues to elude him; it "slips between [his] fingers."

Ponge includes in the text of *Soap* false starts, personal admonitions ("Develop this a little"), directives to "crumple and throw away every note or rough draft." At one point, Ponge decides to send the manuscript to his good friend Albert Camus, whose response to the work is pointedly unfavorable. What does Ponge do with this less-than-lukewarm response? He includes the letter in the text of *Soap*, of course.

What is incredible is the voracity of a mind intent on capturing a vision—if each attempt is a failure, then he fails differently, inventively each time. He fails in a way that makes one reconsider the very definition of failure.

Ponge's *Soap* is not just a document of soap. It is also an argument *for* failure. Failure not as end point, but as process, as dogged, audacious, unrelenting, surprising invention.

And what happens if we think of failure not as end point, not as detour, but as a different kind of unfolding? Failure as experiment? As practice? What if instead of saying we have failed we say that we are failuring? What if a practice of imagination is often also a practice of failure?

•

Her daughter has completed a week at "The Lost City of Atlantis" camp. In which she has constructed a small aquaponics system that includes a design of her own Atlantis and its inhabitants. A fishbowl aquarium with living plants to wrap roots around the city and a small electric pump to aerate the water—the whole thing is designed to create a self-sustaining habitat for plants and guppies.

All week long, the campers worked on their Atlantises, and every night she and the other parents got the report. Mosaics were being constructed around the fishbowl with glass gemstones and pottery shards. Figures and animals were being molded from clay, along with small-scale architectural marvels: hidden chambers, trap doors. When she goes to pick her daughter up from camp each afternoon, the sculptures unfurl from the tables—organic, monumental. The excitement in the workshop is palpable.

She didn't know what to expect when she picked up her daughter on the last day of camp. But when she arrived, she had to laugh. Each Atlantis was utterly different. Each was utterly original. Most were more than three feet tall. One girl had forgone the idea of a living system and simply filled her fishbowl with water and cups of glitter. Her father tottered out to the car while the glitter bunched and swirled like a living creature pummeling the bowl. "How are we supposed to get this home, honey?" he said, but his voice was not without a note of dazed astonishment.

Her daughter's Atlantis is not an Atlantis with cups of glitter—her daughter had wanted the fish too badly. The water is clear; two guppies are swimming in it. The mosaics glint from clay in lozenges of turquoise and cobalt. When they get home, they balance the whole wild monstrosity on her dresser and plug it in. The pump turns on, the water trickles like a fountain, and the guppies happily mouth their little Os. Late at night, she can hear the sound of water dripping in her daughter's room, and she thinks of what it means for her daughter to have manifested something that had only a few days before existed entirely in her imagination.

But when her daughter wakes early the next morning, she finds one of her fish—Flutter—belly up at the top of the water. Her daughter is inconsolable. They call a friend who has a freshwater aquarium. And they gratefully take the remaining living fish over to the friend's house and release it. Then, they perform a funeral outside by the Seville orange tree. Last week, they'd been painting rocks using their Lotería game cards as models. Her daughter chooses two rocks for the grave: LA LUNA (the moon) and EL CORAZÓN (the heart).

After examining the aquarium—the pump, the filter, the temperature of the water—her daughter declares the aquarium does not work the way she dreamed it would, the way it is supposed to. The Lost City is a failure.

•

Her daughter is too young for *Soap*. But what she can understand—at least somewhat—are the films of Jean Painlevé.

Jean Painlevé's films generally defy genre: Created in the 1930s, they are neither science documentaries nor dramas, but hybrid creations meant for both academic and general audiences. With titles like *Shrimp Stories*, *The Love Life of the Octopus*, and *How Some Jellyfish Are Born*, Painlevé's films reveal the hidden worlds of such disparate subjects as vampire bats, shipworms, hermaphrodite mollusks, sea urchins, and clumps of "underwater vegetables" that are, in fact, crabs strolling about in seaweed camouflage.

Her daughter shares her love for marine life, aquaria, and invertebrates of all varieties—especially striped pyjama squid and sea stars. When they make a nest of blankets on the couch and she shows her daughter Painlevé's *Sea Urchins*, she also shows her photos of Painlevé's studio. The tanks and lighting, all of the strange contraptions that he had to envision and invent in order to create his films.

In *The Seahorse*—one of the first films ever using footage shot underwater—Painlevé enclosed his camera in an exquisitely designed waterproof box. The enormous glass aquariums he used to film "shattered on two occasions—once exploding with such force that it flattened a crew member against the wall." Spare parts were corroded by artificial seawater, and when, after waiting thirty-six hours without sleeping, the film crew missed the delivery of the first seahorse, Painlevé created an electrical device to shock himself so he wouldn't miss another. All of that was just for one film. Painlevé and Geneviève Hamon—his partner both in life and in the films—made more than two hundred.

Her admiration of Painlevé hearkens back to the reason that she wanted to study biology in the first place. His desire to capture processes beyond our capacity to see or recognize them (who in the course of their daily life would have been able to view the birth of a jellyfish? The eerily beautiful courtship ballet of sea slugs? The almost hallucinogenic growth of a crystal?) Surreal, incognito, dizzyingly defiant of simple explanation, delighting in both the wonderous and repugnant—Painlevé made us see that science is indeed fiction, the unimaginable real.

But more—his investigations didn't just pull back the curtain on what was more or less invisible to humans. As James Leo Cahill tells us in his book *Zoological Surrealism: The Nonhuman Cinema of Jean Painlevé*, the films of Jean Painlevé developed "a mode of looking and a surreal practice of cinematic encounter that, in turning its attention to animal life and nonhuman world, also critically altered conceptions of human life." In a talk, Cahill goes on to say, "[Painlevé] developed a practice of anthropomorphism without anthropocentrism such that it asks viewers to consider what animals might teach us about being human differently rather than simply how they might reflect our all too human values and foibles."

Painlevé has been described as "[slipping] through the cracks of film history." With the exception of *L'Hippocampe* (*The Seahorse*), his films were never commercial successes. They didn't reach wide distribution—they were considered too volatile and strange. He was scorned by his scientific colleagues; some were outraged at the very idea that cinema could be a valuable tool for science. But it's always Painlevé she thinks of when she and her daughter find themselves practically glued against the glass of the Arizona-Sonora Desert Museum's Warden Aquarium. How patient you must be to see what's actually in front of you. How many times you have to practice seeing. *Teach me to be human differently* may not be the first thing one thinks about when staring through the glass at garden eels, or a seahorse looping its tail around a slim piece of seagrass. But maybe it should be.

•

In *The Queer Art of Failure*, J. Halberstam argues, "The social worlds we inhabit, after all, as so many thinkers have reminded us, are not inevitable; they were not always bound to turn out this way, and what's more, in the process of producing *this* reality, many other realities, fields of knowledge, and ways of being have been discarded and, to cite Foucault again, 'disqualified.'"

Where and how do ideas move? Where and how do they slip from one mind into another, one image speaking to another's deepest longings or lonelinesses? How are ideas lost or found?

She can't stop thinking about these small vignettes: a manuscript of soap, a film about sea urchins. As if they are worlds in miniature. As if she is walking again through that room of Atlantises. As if the imagination and its processes are on display.

She can't stop thinking that a culture allergic to failure is also a culture allergic to imagination.

•

After the Lost City is unplugged, her partner encourages their daughter to keep trying to figure out what went wrong. He tells her how Edison once said, "I have not failed 10,000 times—I've successfully found 10,000 ways that will not work."

While the quote is generally accurate ("Results! [. . .] I have gotten a lot of results! I know several thousand things that won't work!"), the thousands of experiments with different materials relate not to Edison's work on the light bulb, as many assume, but instead on his later work with storage batteries.

Light bulbs or storage batteries; of course, this distinction hardly matters when a dream is dead. As Bachelard tells us: "Even a minor event in the life of a child is an event of that child's world and thus a world event."

Perhaps it is important to mention at this point that Edison did not, in fact, invent the light bulb. He simply refined it—trying filament after filament after filament—until at last, one—made of carbonized bamboo—was able to hold the light much longer than all the rest.

And isn't that what we're looking for? Discovering the things that make it possible to see deeper, to see differently? To feel that one belongs to something unimaginable, a moment that holds the light longer than the rest?

•

This is what she loves most about the work of visual artist Miyanaga Aiko: You are not certain you can trust what you are seeing. A ghostly key resides inside a nearly transparent book; both are encased in a block of clear resin. Other blocks of resin contain different apparitions: clocks, shoes, keys inside a suitcase, a chair. Each sculpture is devoid of color, recognizable only by shape and texture, like a frozen breath or cloud. In the *"waiting for awakening – clock,"* ornate minute and hour hands are just barely visible, scrim written in air.

You know the kind of art she means. The type that situates you in a different experience of time. The kind of thing that makes your whole body crane forward, some kind of electrical circuit stuttering its current from the tips of your toes to your amygdala. That object you now want to possess because it's thrown open some kind of door that's shoved your depressed, disillusioned self back to curiosity, back to life.

And how does one make such a thing, a thing to defy seeing? Miyanaga's sculptures are made of naphthalene—the substance used for mothballs. She encloses naphthalene forms in blocks of resin, and drills a tiny hole that allows oxygen to enter. Over time, the naphthalene sublimates. Surfaces frost over, tiny crystals appear, some of the objects fragment and then disintegrate/disappear completely. Miyanaga says they "shift not as fast as melting ice, or as slowly as a weathering Greek sculpture." Forms that are white will eventually turn clear—the moment, Miyanaga describes, they "awaken from sleep." Miyanaga's sculptures contain shoes, clocks, suitcases, chairs—"impression[s] of something already used, something that holds time." Her sculptures transform the real, the ordinary, into the unimaginable.

The sublimated objects fail to hold their shapes. But this failure is failure as the possibility of time's reframing. Failure as an alternative to chronological time. (If naphthalene was again placed in the mold, the shapes would reappear, then disintegrate again, over and over.)

It's all she realizes she's ever wanted. To make something that keeps someone up at night, their heart buzzing like a bird's. After she first saw Miyanaga's work, she lay awake on her couch thinking of alternative modes of time—modes in which pasts and futures might exist simultaneously or inversely or in a way that defies language and description. And art that might capture that. That such an imagining might at first seem to be a failure due to its nonsensical and counterintuitive presentation. Such a vision might, at first glance, appear to be a failure because it seems an unwieldy, unrecognizable, even somewhat spectral mess. But that such a creation might later be understood as a breakthrough, a revelation.

•

Her favorite writing workshop she's ever attended was taught by Sueyeun Juliette Lee and titled "That Forward Trajectory: Poems from the Future." She remembers the night Lee taught the workshop she showed up despite battling a bad cold.

The required readings were like unwrapping a star on your birthday. An NPR article on predictive technologies. Raymond Williams's chapter "The City and the Future." FM-2030's *Are You a Transhuman*, and more. A rewatching of *La Jetée*. She reads notes she'd scrawled across one of Lee's poems: *Human possibility can expand through different convolutions of language and other modes of "presence" and "inhabiting."*

In that workshop and in a subsequent interview, Lee spoke of the role of imagination: "The speculative is the only way we can have a vision for the future, because the circumstances of our collective lives right now strive to tell us the world can never be any other way. To have fantasy, to dream, to have righteousness or hope, we must open ourselves to the speculative, we must summon its transgressive-ness and non-conformity into us. I always felt that to really be an artist of any stripe was to rehabilitate the human imagination, to intervene in it. And what we see when we see injustice is a failure of the imagination."

It was partly because of Sueyeun Juliette Lee's workshop that she began to write a novel inspired by a speculative future—one in which the future of species loss could be more directly experienced and imagined.

•

In the book she's written that is her failuring is a scene where the two lovers first see footage of the sun rising over the Rioja mountains and disturbing a flock of migrating flamingos that lift their wings in the air. At the time of the viewing (set in the future), flamingos have been extinct for many years, and the recently discovered footage is rare.

> Somewhere around the middle of the lecture, the lights were dimmed to stream some archived 3D footage from the Laguna Brava Nature Preserve, a saltwater lagoon high in the Argentinian Andes. A landscape in muddy, predawn colors rose before us, mist swathing the landscape like steam rising from a rag soaked in boiling water. Salt crusts flanked the lake edges in ribbons of pale and gritty gray-brown, colors that corresponded precisely to that particular sensation when life feels flat and dull and has the texture of wet cardboard. It seemed a desolate expanse, scrubbed of life and color.
> Then suddenly, it changed.
> We watched as sunrise spilled over the distant orange and blue edges of the La Rioja Mountains and small ripples

on the lake began to coruscate with sunlight. There was absolute silence, the light advancing quickly, the scene panning to the left. That's when we saw them. Hundreds of Andean flamingos, previously hidden from view, lifted their wings with the dawn in a great wave of pink.

When I saw her, often when I think of her, I think of that moment. How everyone in that darkened auditorium gasped. How she slipped her hand into mine and clutched it to her breastbone, the air around me seeming to rush beneath my skin. We stared down into those beating wings and I felt a sudden wave of dizziness, my heart thudding from a long way off, as if it had been wrapped in cotton and set adrift on some distant continent.

Sometimes when she finds herself awake at night, she thinks of this moment. A moment whose making created some different space inside of her. Like her friend describing some essays he loved—that somehow you're looking around like you do every day, but suddenly your eye catches some impossible shiny object. Some secret bright thing.

It mattered that much to her—the idea of having people *feel* the weight of species loss. Those hours spent. That maybe she doesn't know now what that failure will become but trusts that that space will engender something. Perhaps this essay. Perhaps something else.

Because to think of failure differently—as unmaking and remaking, not knowing, and dismantling—may be part of a creative process that yields more surprising and generous ways of being in the world. To see imagination as a practice to be honored and cultivated. To understand that part of the reason we are living our current sixth extinction and climate crisis is perhaps because we have failed both in our practices of failure *and* imagination.

So what is the alternative? Halberstam encourages us to ask. To consider failure as process means to consider a mode that revels in detours, celebrates the unexpected, upsets hierarchical and/or established modes of knowing. And "to articulate an alternative vision of life, love, and labor, and to put such a vision into practice."

So that the detour, the experiment, is, in fact, also arrival.

Not just for the ornithologists, the ecologists, the sculptors, the poets. It is a call to arms for all to the realm of the speculative, the as-yet-unimagined, the as-yet-unrealized possible.

•

At the moment, her daughter's grief is too fresh. She does not want to build another aquarium, or shape another Atlantis. But the way one can work with a glass jar is still fresh in her daughter's mind.

And so, instead of making a replacement Atlantis, her daughter makes her son a night-light because the other night-lights have failed him. Takes a mason jar and turns it on its side. She paints it green, but a kind of pale translucent green, then hot glues several glow-in-the-dark dinosaurs on top and puts a small string of LED lights inside. "It has to be a different kind of night-light," she explains, "because T. has a different kind of fear of the dark these days."

Later, long after her daughter has gone to bed, she walks by her son's room and sees it glowing there like something living and bioluminescent, full of a kind of beautiful calm.

Gardens

SHIBAKI YOSHIKO

Dear Shibaki Yoshiko,

These days, I spend a lot of time in my backyard, digging rainwater basins, fertilizing citrus trees, watering the scrappy baby pomegranates. It's not (yet) a particularly beautiful backyard—there's a lot of bare dirt and sprawling cactus patches, and the kids like to dig holes and bury things, so the garden tools are often strewn about. But there is a giant eucalyptus complete with tree house, and a little drought-tolerant fruit tree orchard we've been coaxing to life. Sometimes, I'll climb up and look at the moon from the tree house, or I'll walk out and see that overnight, the plum tree has burst into blossom on its largest branch, or that the baby desert tortoises have ventured out into the sunshine, and are munching on a few desert willow flowers.

Gardens are like Rube Goldberg machines with their sunlight and earthworms and leafcutter ants invisibly turning things over into soil and blossoms, fruit and butterfly chrysalises. It's the quietness of gardens that makes me think of your work, so after I've been outside for a while, I'll come back in and take out your teapot and make some tea. It's an old Kutani teapot—fragile, hand-painted with gold—where two women in intricately patterned lavender and rust-striped kimonos look out onto a misty garden.

I love in your story "Ripples" when your narrator, Takako, who is busy caretaking her ailing mother, lets us glimpse her interior world: "Lately she'd gotten into the habit of dreaming the impossible whenever she felt overwhelmed by life or by her ties to other people. In the morning, for instance, when she opened her eyes and parted the curtains, she imagined that she was living on the third floor of a large, comfortable apartment building with flowers on a sunlit terrace. Turning around, she would see a man still asleep in the dark inner bedroom [. . .]. 'How wonderful,' she'd think, 'I'm married!'"

Every time I read this story, I'm affected by this moment. Does it echo your own life since you had to leave your studies to support your mother and two younger sisters after your father died? I can't help but wonder how the narrative echoes another question: What allows women to thrive when they feel trapped, especially by the banality of the domestic? Or what allows us to access a source of resilience in order to at least function within such circumstances? I'm moved by Takako's response to what I imagine would be the sometimes quietly suffocating moments of a life bound by familial obligation. She "dream[s] the impossible."

I'm not sure I would say it's a lonely task to find one's form of resistance, mostly because I think that it's a necessary thing, so maybe the loneliness is just part of the equation. But I know what it means to find, in the mundane routine of everyday life, some kind of encouragement. The gentle insistence of someone reminding you, look here, it's important to realize that there are many ways of being in the world. That you have a choice.

Which has to do with the second part of what I love about the story—when the real estate agent shows up at Takako's house and tells the family that he's tracked them down to pay them for a parcel of land the deceased father had purchased years before. You were brilliant to make it both ordinary and unexpected, and your writing is seamless—we understand it wasn't the agent's job to find the family. And you make it clear that had he not done so, they would most likely have never known about the land or its value.

It's in this act that the title of the story "Ripples" begins to resonate. Because even though Takako's family gets greedily caught up in the windfall of the land's sale (and to a certain extent, even Takako—who earns a meager salary at a university library—is affected), something has shifted for her, and for the real estate agent as well. I appreciate when Takako visits the land and is moved by its surprising beauty; she is also moved by the agent's determination to find her family.

One of my favorite moments is when she visits his office to thank him: "Takako drew her parcel closer. Ever since the agent had located her family, she had been completely absorbed in selling the land, but now, finally, she was able to come and thank him. The gift was only a symbol of the gratitude that she alone seemed to feel. A look of surprise flitted across the man's face. Searching for someone for three months had been a remarkable experience, but he'd never expected any of them to make a courtesy call afterward. He gazed at the department-store package that Takako handed over." He then tells her, "It was only my job," but she disagrees. "I think what you did was extraordinary."

The story has preoccupied me lately because I have been thinking a lot about individual responses that counteract the usual narratives, that, in one way or another, resist the pressure of conformity. And the ripple effects such responses can have. And about our contemporary moment, such a strange and disorienting time for so many reasons, but one of them being the sixth extinction crisis—an issue so colossal and abstract it seems nearly impossible to try to engage with as an individual, much less a species. And yet.

And yet I read about a person in Cambridgeshire, England, who was so disturbed by the frantic cries of swifts trying to find nesting spots that had disappeared, that he built more than thirty thousand swift nesting boxes in his garage. And another person in Oxfordshire who, after realizing hedgehog numbers were plummeting because of private, walled-off garden enclosures, created the longest hedgehog superhighway in the world. (It's constructed of holes in stone garden walls, tiny staircases, and wooden ramps, so hedgehogs no longer have to risk crossing busy roads to roam.)

There are brides in Hong Kong spearheading efforts to forgo shark fin soup as a traditional wedding menu delicacy (the soup is made of fins sliced from still-living sharks that are then tossed back into the sea to drown). And a group of volunteer divers in New Zealand that gets together on weekends to remove ghost nets—lost and discarded fishing nets that trap and kill seabirds and marine life—from the sea. There's a scientist in Indonesia's Mahakam River working with local fishermen to attach acoustic devices to nets that prevent river dolphin entanglements. And a teenager in Delhi so disturbed by a video of a plastic straw being painfully extracted from an olive ridley sea turtle's nostril, he's worked tirelessly to eliminate millions of plastic straws in the hospitality industry.

Like the estate agent demonstrates in your story, sometimes extraordinary acts are simply what a person decides to do because they've stopped long enough to pay attention and quietly come up with their own response.

Our house and yard have been neglected for decades. As I plant the chuparosa and sage and mesquite trees, and set up little apartments for the native bees, I think of the others that will live here next—the people and the yellow-rumped warblers, Anna's hummingbirds, and lesser goldfinches—and how their lives, because of these acts, will be able to intersect. I like thinking that what I plant in this place will likely outlast me.

I'll pour some tea and think of how resistance can mean something as simple as generosity in ordinary circumstances, and how small acts can move through the lives of other beings in remarkable ways. I see it in that moment of the story before Takako leaves the agent's office. "Though thinking it was bad to keep a man away from his work, she decided to stay for a few more minutes. She would never see him again, and for her as for him, this moment seemed very precious." That last line was so quietly and unexpectedly moving; I felt its delicacy, and how authentically it captured the supple spark of human connection.

Even when I first saw the teapot sitting on a dusty shelf in the thrift store, it always seemed important to me that two people were looking together at the garden. That whatever they were gazing at inside the mist—pond or orchard, complicated past or blurry future—could be shared. That perhaps one person's way of seeing could inspire the other's.

There's something else painted on the teapot: the moon in various phases of its cycle. And a whole host of tiny gold stars. Circling past the edges of the window the women gaze from as if they're saying, don't worry, when the sun's light fails, we'll stay here with you until you're ready to turn away, the gold of one star's light rippling each to another.

> With gratitude and admiration,
> Katherine

My Monster, Your Monster, Our Monster

Dear Godzilla,

It's summer, and the kids and I are about to go swimming at ES's pool. Last time we went, I'd just lifted the skimmer from the wall to net some leaves when I saw the lizard at the bottom. A desert spiny lizard, belly-up with those unmistakable streaks of blue iridescence. The drowned lizards unnerve me. And, of course, they make me think of you.

Lately, I've been rewatching your movies, especially the ones where you go on a rampage and really make a mess. You singeing Hong Kong's coastline to burnt marshmallow, ripping the Golden Gate Bridge apart like a wind-up toy. Crumpling the Atami Castle like cardboard and liquifying power lines with your atomic breath. That shrieking roar! Skyscrapers sliced through like sticks of butter! The scale of destruction (that one knows is safely cinematic), and you, on the ruins of Fenway Park, throwing your head back and bellowing into a sky seared orange with tufted clouds of radiation. Susan Sontag knew it too: "Thus the science fiction film [. . .] is concerned with the aesthetics of destruction, with the peculiar beauties to be found in wreaking havoc." And: "There is nothing," she says, "like the thrill of watching all those expensive sets come tumbling down." I don't care if buildings crumple like obvious papier-mâché; I don't care that sometimes your rubber monster suit creases or that your eyes go googly in ways that no person on this planet would describe as natural—the beauty is watching how quickly it all unravels, the utter relinquishing of power and control.

Sontag wrote that essay, "The Imagination of Disaster," in 1965, but you wouldn't believe how relevant it is today. Or how much I appreciate the fact that she clearly spent hours of her life in front of campy midcentury sci-fi films. Though, of course, she's the one who can articulate their cultural relevance, what they signified. Also, I shouldn't say campy—some of those films are brilliant.

I've been preoccupied by something your own Professor Hayashida said (forgive me for sliding back to 1985): "When mankind falls into conflict with nature, monsters are born." Here's what's troubling me: I knew in general terms that you were an allegory: both the casualty and incarnation of American thermonuclear testing. *In 1954, a gigantic, prehistoric sea creature was awakened after its underwater ecosystem was irradiated, etc.* And I always did love that you represented more than just a simple monstrosity or slapstick source of entertainment.

But I didn't know that those original scenes of destruction were images meant to echo the bombing of Japanese cities in WWII. You, stomping through the inferno and debris, sirens blaring, the wounded spilling out of the hospitals, everyone in a shared, communal state of panic. You represented the cumulative horror of the atomic bomb, the scar on the Japanese psyche. Even your colossal size was meant to be representative of the scale of the trauma. The film historian David Kalat writes: "The entire fabric of Godzilla is woven from the threads of real horror, human suffering, and apocalypse on a global scale."

I'd never actually seen the original 1954 *Gojira* film. Now that I have, there's a moment I can't forget: When the camera pans to a little girl whose small body sends the Geiger counter stuttering—her very body the source of radiation. You were born a collective nightmare, the monster who told us we had to listen to our monsters. Now I've learned this about you, I can't ever unlearn it.

I never watched you as a kid; my parents wouldn't have been interested in Godzilla movies. I won't mince it: They would have found you ridiculous. But they were the ones that ultimately taught me to see you in your complexity.

My mother, for example. Because of the way she cared for nonhuman creatures: attentively, steadfastly. Not just our guppies and loaches in the aquarium at home, our dog and cat, but in her classroom as well. Because of my mother, schoolchildren fell in love with guinea pigs, a Madagascar hissing cockroach, a Mexican redknee tarantula. Learned about rainforests by building an entire paper biome in their classroom that stretched from ceiling to floor.

Joy—the tarantula—my mother kept that spider alive for almost twenty-five years.

And visiting my dad's office when I was growing up. A forestry professor, his office was crammed with marvelous objects: sugar pine cones as long as my arm, huge cross sections of ringed tree trunks, labeled samples of tropical woods: zebrawood and purpleheart and cocobolo. He taught me that the biological world was full of astonishments beyond what I could imagine.

Now anthropologists and evolutionary biologists have noticed that you're getting bigger. In their *Science* paper titled "A movie monster evolves, fed by fear," authors Nathaniel J. Dominy and Ryan Calsbeek show that you have "doubled in size since 1954," your inexplicable growth quite possibly "evolving in response to a spike in humanity's collective anxiety" and "the idea," the authors mention, "that climate change is now the mother of all security problems." (I can't help but think of Margaret Atwood: "I think calling it climate change is rather limiting. I would rather call it the everything change.")

Did you watch the Tuvalu foreign minister giving his COP26 speech while standing at his podium? You only realize when the camera pans out that he's nearly thigh-deep in seawater, speaking in suit and tie, the blue background and flags behind him just scrappy patches of fabric against the water that engulfs him on all sides. "We cannot wait for speeches," he says, "when the sea is rising around us all the time." (I couldn't help it; part of me wanted you to make an appearance behind him, a few serrated plates slicing through the water—but more on that later.)

For now, I watch you stomp across the screen late at night while binge eating whatever stash of candy my children have left above the fridge. And I track you down in *Science*, and in pandemic talks from film-studies institutions. And I dog-ear the pages of *Godzilla on My Mind* and *A Critical History and Filmography of Toho's Godzilla Series*. And I can't help but suggest to new parents that they should consider reading Randall E. Osborne's short essay "Godzilla as a Parenting Tool" from *The Official Godzilla Compendium*.

And yes, I'm still moved every time I see Mothra burning into ashes, saving your life.

You know what I appreciated about *Godzilla: King of the Monsters*? The movie posits the messy idea that monsters are meant to coexist with humans. That communication is even possible. Godzilla, in the end, belongs to the human species the way all species on this planet belong to each other. Of course, other aspects of the movie are problematic—the abdication of human responsibility, that ecoterrorism is the alternative to annihilation, that destruction is the only path to restore balance to the natural world. But I see Serizawa sacrificing his own life to save yours, reaching out a trembling hand to touch your skin. (I won't lie; I watched the movie alone so I could cry without my kids making fun of me.) Because I know something that they don't. As William Tsutsui reminds us, "Even Godzilla's skin, thick and furrowed like the keloid scars that afflicted the survivors of Hiroshima and Nagasaki, evoked the agony of irradiation." And, of course, also because of what Serizawa says: "Goodbye, old friend."

Your presence has become unusually complex: You're a monster and a savior, an enemy and defender, a commentary on scientific progress and environmentalism, a menacing figure and an impetus for change. We can't reckon with the current crisis if we're still telling ourselves that it doesn't exist. I pick up the "burning Godzilla" latex figure on my desk. Did you know the latest bushfire season in Australia killed more than a billion animals? I hold you and think of the koalas burning. I'll say that again: koalas burning to death. There's even a name for it: solastalgia—the emotional or existential distress caused by environmental change.

The kids—they're tired of me sitting at this desk. They have their pool toys. They want to go swimming.

But first, listen—you'd like this moment from Tawada Yōko's *Where Europe Begins*. The narrator tells about a village girl whose mother is sick with an incurable illness. One day, a white serpent appears and tells her that she must undertake a difficult journey, but that her mother can be cured. The girl protests when she learns that she has to cross the mountains—the mountains, she tells the serpent, are inhabited by monsters. "You needn't be afraid of them," the white serpent explains. "When you see them, just remember that you, too, like all other human beings, were once a monster in one of your previous lives."

I thought you'd like that. The part about us all at one time being real monsters, each of us. Especially little girls.

Speaking of which, V. and I watched *Spirited Away* for the first time together—I'd forgotten the arresting strangeness of its spirits and creatures, how universally it speaks while also defying easy explanation. There's something that Miyazaki says about the movie that strikes me as relevant: "I created a heroine who is an ordinary girl, someone with whom the audience can sympathize. It's not a story in which the characters grow up, but a story in which they draw on something already inside them, brought out by the particular circumstances. I want my young friends to live like that, and I think they, too, have such a wish."

Here's my wish: For you to be transformed into the minds of others as you have been in mine. For a collective nightmare to catalyze collective action. I want a new you, a sky-blue Godzilla, that can represent engagement across continents, languages, countries. Sontag says in her essay that "a great enough disaster cancels all enmities." I want the monstrous to be awoken in service of addressing a new nightmare, for the collective unconscious to rise up, for an icon to be recognized again for what it was dreamed to be in the first place—both warning and an impetus for change. Not just my Godzilla or your Godzilla. *Our* Godzilla.

When I was sixteen, my father moved our family to Costa Rica for his sabbatical. One weekend, we'd been camping in Monteverde Cloud Forest; I was sharing a tent with my brother. After dinner, dusk had fallen, and we'd been walking back to the camp. The jungled rainforest trees were in silhouette; the creaturely noises enveloped us. And then the fireflies began to blink on, lighting up the dark in the thousands, layer upon layer, until I found myself with my head thrown back, afloat in the dense, flashing swarms.

If I'd been aware in the previous moments that I possessed a body that swung its legs and arms in response to a particular gravity, that awareness had fled. I was a speck afloat in an ocean of bioluminescence. I might as well have had a thousand eyes, a thousand flung-open apertures to apprehend that vast, pulsing matrix of stuttering light instead of two.

It's something to feel dwarfed by wonder. Which, let's be clear, can be terror too. To feel in awe of a presence so immense that one is left speechless.

This time, what we face is less visible, and less accessible to human imagination and experience. This time you are a monster of ruin and erasures so universal and yet so subtly interconnected you are difficult for us to fully see.

When I worked at the field station in Mexico, I coordinated a marine biology camp for kids. It was July and humid, and a squall had driven hundreds of toxic blue Portuguese man o' war into the shallows and on the beach; the children couldn't swim or tide pool. So I drove the campers to another beach, where they spotted something unusual in the surf: a Risso's dolphin. It was about twelve feet long, its skin a kind of mottled pewter, its snub nose making it look like a miniature pilot whale. It was so newly dead that it actually pained me to see its body collide with the reef, see the rocks scraping away its skin. To better show the campers, I wrapped my arms around the strange, slick body, and braced myself against the shifting sand that sucked at my feet.

In my recurring dream, I'm there again with my campers, my arms still cradling the tensile, silvery head. But there's a moment when the rocking waters grow inexplicably calm. And the children look up, squinting at the horizon. The seawater is suddenly full of flashing green Jell-O molds that bob just under the surface, somehow alive. And I read it on their faces first, that unnameable mixture of awe and dread. I know you're coming. Though I always wake up just before seeing you, wake up just as I've let the dolphin fall out of my arms and am turning my head.

I'm telling you this because the dream ends there. It isn't clear what happens next. Which version of you—which Godzilla—is rising? The monster that's coming to destroy us, or the one that represents the collective refusal to let this epoch of damage continue—the monster that sets us free?

Love,
Katherine

The Twilight World

It's twilight and her neighbor is slipping into his swimming pool because the lights have just flicked on in palm trees above her backyard fence, and the dog walkers are sliding out of their houses testing the still-sizzling asphalt with their own bare feet. It's twilight and the two coyotes with mange come trotting by then lean into shadows of the velvet mesquite trees, and she feels it—the contours of something waiting, something about to arrive. Twilight is the whisper world, like driving in the desert at night when your radio catches some clear ribbon of music unspooling from somewhere invisible, then loses it, and you can't help but hold your breath you're listening so hard—the static skating across the skin of your arms in dusky anticipation.

Izumi Kyōtarō writes about twilight and the twilight world. "Twilight," he says, "is neither the color of night nor the color of darkness. [. . .] neither simply a sensation of day, nor of light. In the momentary boundary of entering darkness from light, is that not where the twilight world lies?"

This evening she's been scrolling through pictures of the wildfires in Maui on her phone. The gray slumps of abandoned cars, spiked palm trees blackened to char. Ash crawling over the ruins like a singed animal trying its best to cover the wounds of the landscape, the loved ones still lost under debris, trying to smooth it all out, reconcile its horror, and she can almost smell it through the screen, the singed plastic smell of smoldering homes—homes, not houses—noxious, chemical.

In Gerald Figal's introduction to *Civilization and Monsters: Spirits of Modernity in Meiji Japan* he excerpts Izumi Kyōtarō's passage on twilight, then mentions: "As anyone familiar with Japanese folk motifs knew, to invoke twilight was also to invite bakemono (monsters, literally 'changing things') onto the stage of discourse."

Lately, she's been feeling like she's living in a twilight world. A place where we're standing in the doorway that shimmers between darkness and light, just waiting for the monsters to show up.

•

That afternoon, on the verge of twilight, she drove out to the auto salvage lot at the edge of the city for a reclaimed bumper for her old Toyota. The sky was one of those near-molten, hold-your-breath technicolor sunsets Arizona is famous for, except she couldn't stop thinking how the Maui sky had looked like this, like clouds torn apart and lashed with lava. When she got to the salvage yard, there were men among the mangled cars pulling apart and hosing down their greasy innards, and the August heat was stifling, like being boiled in the very air itself, and she couldn't help but think, irrationally, the embery sky was actually a wildfire in the distance howling its way toward her to consume her and the men and the disemboweled cars, and she noticed how oddly calm she felt in the certainty of that unmaking, the certainty that yes, of course this was it, the actual end of the world.

She has to transition this essay from the third person to the first. She has to get the monsters closer.

To shift from she to I. She does this by thinking of the Japanese women writers she's been reading. Lately, she's been writing them letters. It's a way to show how their writing has changed her; by evoking their presence, she affirms their work is now alive in her too. When she writes to them, I am no longer standing outside of my body, looking in.

•

Lately, I've been having a recurring dream about being a cyborg with a glass aquarium implanted inside my chest. The dream started a few months ago, when my mother had her stroke. In the dream, my aquarium is full of murky water, and when I unbutton my shirt and look at myself in the mirror, the light inside it glows green, and my heart squishes against the back glass like a muscled, dark fish. There are scraps of seaweeds inside, and something living that shuffles in the mealy gloom, striped, like an extra-large kuhli loach, the same eellike fish my mother kept in our aquarium when we were little. She never let the aquarium get overgrown then. But the stroke has affected the right side of her body. It's clear in the dream that my aquarium is getting murkier and murkier. I'm afraid the fish will die. I don't know how to clean my own aquarium. I am unprepared.

The stories from Maui began to trickle into the news. Two women on vacation spent hours hunkered down in the hotel pool, the building eclipsed by an incandescent wall of flame. Another stood on the overpass watching her mother's house burn, not knowing if her mother was still inside. Some ran into the ocean, swimming farther when cars began exploding. Some saw the ocean itself catch fire.

When I pick up my worn copy of Gaston Bachelard's *The Psychoanalysis of Fire*, thinking there might be something to glean for this essay, I feel ridiculous when I read the first line. He begins, "We have only to speak of an object to think that we are being objective. But, because we chose it in the first place, the object reveals more about us than we do about it."

•

I'm looking at a view of the San Francisco Peaks outside my mother's rehab hospital. The mountain rises stately, substantive. But I notice there's a patch that's still raw from the past year's wildfires. Fires so fierce they thought they might have to evacuate the city. There's a hush in the scorch of that space that belongs to the twilight world too.

When I wake up for the last few nights in my childhood bedroom, I try scrolling through pictures on my phone of midcentury modern houses in Palm Springs. There's something calming about their parsing geometries, their gilded sputnik chandeliers and color-saturated doors—aqua and acid pink and tangerine—that whisper *welcome, nostalgic dreamer, here's your martini, let's just shove these ash-covered bodies into the shadows and step outside on cool cement pavers, see these tidy rows of golden barrel cacti, you can rest out here by the pool, let the chlorine smell erase the fumes with its antiseptic perfume*—and even if the whole thing is spectacle and utterly imagined, my anxieties are poured into preformed shapes and riotous rectangles of color, and these two-dimensional images of houses, which do not belong to me, nor ever will, make my imagination light up like tiny sparklers on a birthday cake, and no, my dear, nothing's burning, it's just the match being blown out, and thus anesthetized, I can slip back to sleep.

Nostalgia, solastalgia—they both share the Greek root *algos*, which means pain.

•

Lately, my son has been obsessed with Pokémon. I loved discovering that Pokémon, in Japanese, is short for "pocket monsters." He reads the colorful Pokémon cards out loud, telling me of imaginary monsters with extraordinary gifts—monsters that create their own electricity, monsters with ultrasonic hearing, monsters that feast on dreams while patterns on their bodies gleam.

But when I read my son the Pokémon cards, I think of real creatures—of the echolocation powers of inch-long bumblebee bats in Thailand (*Craseonycteris thonglongyai*), the tendriled blue sea dragon sea slug (*Glaucus atlanticus*), which feasts on stinging creatures and stores their cells within its own tissue to defend against predators. Of the eyespots on the hind wings of Io moths (*Automeris io*), which can be covered by their forewings and then flashed open to startle predators. Or of bioluminescent ghost fungus (*Omphalotus nidiformis*) that glows in neon layers from the trunks of dead and dying trees.

In their introduction to *Arts of Living on a Damaged Planet*, the authors tell me: "Our monsters and ghosts help us notice landscapes of entanglement, bodies with other bodies, time with other times."

I wanted to study biology because I realized there were real monsters in the place that I actually lived.

•

All the news is about wildfires, and all my dreams are about contaminated water—algaed aquaria, sewage-strewn streets, rivers clotted with mounds of dead and dying eels.

Until I have a dream that combines both: I'm standing in a group with other aquarium-implanted cyborgs in the middle of the street, and we're surrounded by flames advancing with a menacing sputter. It suddenly dawns on us—all at the same time, I think—that the only water left is in the aquariums we carry, and to use it to try to put out the flames will likely kill us and those creatures we hold inside of us.

I dislike logically incoherent but emotionally charged dreams. Were we all going to die, swallowed up in flames, then spat out into little floating bits of ash? Were some of us supposed to sacrifice ourselves so that others might live? These seem like realistic questions. Also—if we were all going to die anyway, why care so much about the beings that inhabited our aquaria?

But the dream's logic was different. The dream's logic was atmospheric. There was an aura of fragility. And tenderness. And futility. And what we held inside us—the water *and* the creatures—we understood without speaking, were infinitely precious.

•

There's a story my mother used to read me when I was a girl. A Japanese folktale about a woman who loses a dumpling in a crack in the earth, and when she tumbles down it herself, is captured and held prisoner by wicked oni. The oni—monsters—I know were meant to be fierce with their gristly green bodies and three eyes. But secretly I loved them and loved the chunky stone pagodas where they lived, tucked inside the ruined cavern with its trailing tree roots and inconclusive staircases, and lanterns scattered throughout like massive, magical orbs of bright confetti, suffusing the whole scene with the vital green radiance of the mythic and vegetable worlds.

I remember loving how the oni could drink all the water from the river and hold it in their mouths, perhaps forever, or at least until something made them laugh and they unleashed it.

But it's impossible to hold things forever. Just like it was impossible to write a card to my mother on the Mother's Day after her stroke. I don't remember what I actually wrote. But what I wanted to write was, Oh my god, you didn't die, thank god you didn't die, I'm not ready for you to die, not now, not ever.

•

When I was cast in the middle school play, I was disappointed to be Lucy Westenra. It meant I had to spend most of my time running around in a ridiculous, high-necked nightgown pretending to be fragile and beautiful and tragic. But I didn't want to be any of these things. I wanted to be feral and feared. I wanted to be monstrous. I wanted to be Dracula.

My favorite part of the play was when Lucy turns into a vampire, and her fiancé, determined to liberate her, starts to hammer a stake into her heart. That's when I could lash out, flail around in the coffin, scream.

Here's what it felt like to be the monster: I didn't have to be afraid anymore. I didn't have to be afraid of anything. As a monster, I could choose.

Yesterday's twilight found me walking over to my neighbor's house with vintage bathroom tiles to see if the mint green tiles I'd ordered to repair my bathroom matched theirs, and I got caught in a microburst, and the sky was suddenly all hot neons with smoky little arrows of lavender, and a poor hawk was trying to knife its way through the tousled currents, and I thought the heavy limbs of the Aleppo pine might literally be torn from their trunk, but it was thrilling to be out there in the dense thick of it, not dreaming it, not staring from the imaginary window of a Palm Springs house, but skin aching, senses feral, caught in the living elemental rush and tangle.

•

A mother in my daughter's book club has an aquarium she wants to give away, and I leap at the chance to pick it up from her and almost immediately find myself maniacally researching how many parts bleach I need to use to sterilize river rocks and what kind of lighting java moss and duckweed need to thrive. And I suddenly realize how desperate I am to stop having the aquarium dreams, how much I want to materialize the abstract in real life so that its troublesome murk can be scrubbed from my dream life. But even as I'm planting the aquatic plants, testing the pH of the water, and setting in the little floating thermometer, I know it's not the point; it's really not the point at all.

The Fox News reporters were quick to emphasize the Maui fires were caused by downed power lines, not climate change. At the same time, writers in *The New York Times* pointed out that "declining rainfall, rising temperatures, and invasive species"—all proven effects of climate change—had "turned lush Hawaii into a tinderbox," leaving the island more vulnerable to the blaze.

It seems a ridiculous argument. After all, the wildfires in Maui remind me of the wildfires in California remind me of the wildfires in Greece and in Siberia remind me of the wildfires in

Australia, where tens of thousands of koalas were burned alive in their eucalyptus forests—

Bodies of loved ones. Bodies of trees. Bodies of koalas. Bodies of the twilight world.

What are we waiting for in the shimmer? And how are we supposed to live alongside the backdrop of all that's awash in flame?

•

There is a theory that stories involving oni were common during times in Japan marked by famine and disease. It explained why people suddenly disappeared: Oni from another world had simply taken them and fled.

And what if the theory is right, that there is another world—or at least another kind of world? I'm tired of watching dialogue unfold in binaries: us/them, human/nature. I'm tired of waiting for the next wildfires and glacier funerals, of teaching my children words like critically endangered and ecocide. Instead, I want to think of how Izumi taught me to see twilight: as a subtle world of in-betweens. How he believed that there's a whole range of perceiving in general, a more plentiful and nuanced set of possibilities. Which to me means not just for our present time, but for our future.

Even when I was young, I was never able to conceptualize the idea of "Heaven" or "Paradise." But if I have to, I can sketch in my mind another world—a green place where both oni and humans sit, eating together at an enormous stone table. Not in an air of fear or punishment. But something more expansive, with some shared sense of forgiveness and flexibility and inquisitiveness.

I imagine wefts of cool air, a carpet of soft moss beneath our feet, and laughter, probably, at our shared monstrousness. My mother would be there, too, being toasted by the bakemono and the more-than-human creatures she's always cared for, and my father, surrounded by the trees he's spent his life teaching others to recognize, and in that particular twilight world, I see the whole scene lit by lights that flicker inside stones that may be living themselves, and in the dark it's almost familiar, a dream that is not just my own, but one that maybe more than one of us has dreamed, or will dream, and remember.

Additional Reading

Kurahashi, Yumiko. "The Monastery." In *The Shōwa Anthology: Modern Japanese Short Stories*, edited by Van C. Gessel and Tomone Matsumoto, 232–45. Translated by Carolyn Haynes. Tokyo: Kodansha International, Ltd., 1992.

Tawada, Yōko. "Where Europe Begins." In *The Columbia Anthology of Modern Japanese Literature Vol. 2: From 1945 to the Present*, edited by J. Thomas Rimer and Van C. Gessel, 698–711. Translated from German by Susan Bernofsky. New York: Columbia University Press, 2007.

Ōba, Minako. "The Pale Fox." In *The Shōwa Anthology: Modern Japanese Short Stories*, edited by Van C. Gessel and Tomone Matsumoto, 351–61. Translated by Stephen W. Kohl. Tokyo: Kodansha International, Ltd., 1992.

Ōta, Yōko. "Residues of Squalor." In *Japanese Women Writers: Twentieth Century Short Fiction*, translated and edited by Noriko Mizuta Lippit and Kyoko Iriye Selden, 58–83. Armonk, NY: M. E. Sharpe, Inc., 1991.

Taeko, Kōno. "Crabs." In *Rabbits, Crabs, Etc.: Stories by Japanese Women*, translated and edited by Phyllis Birnbaum, 99–131. Honolulu: University of Hawaii Press, 1982.

Tsushima, Yūko. "That One Glimmering Point of Light." In *The Columbia Anthology of Modern Japanese Literature Vol. 2: From 1945 to the Present*, edited by J. Thomas Rimer and Van C. Gessel, 711–23. Translated by Van C. Gessel. New York: Columbia University Press, 2007.

Shibaki, Yoshiko. "Ripples." In *The Shōwa Anthology: Modern Japanese Short Stories*, edited by Van C. Gessel and Tomone Matsumoto, 331–50. Translated by Michael C. Brownstein. Tokyo: Kodansha International, Ltd., 1992.

Acknowledgments

Grateful acknowledgment is made to the editors of the publications in which these essays first appeared:

Terrain.org: "Kintsugi: Art of Repair"
DIAGRAM: "My Monster, Your Monster, Our Monster"
Flyway: "Microseasons: Selections"
Wild Roof Journal: "The Crane Wife"
On the Seawall: "Soap: Art of Failure"
River Teeth: "Wedding of the Foxes"

Deepest gratitude to Daniel Slager, Lauren Langston Klein, Mike Corrao, Bailey Hutchinson, Mary Austin Speaker, and all of the wonderfully passionate and supportive staff at Milkweed Editions. My deep gratitude to Tirzah Goldenberg for her marvelous editing skills. Special thanks to Fady Joudah for his dazzling mind, poems, and friendship.

I am indebted to William H. Schlesinger, David Fischer, Rick Ostfeld, Claudia Rosen, Shannon LaDeau, Steward Pickett, and the late Gary Lovett of the Cary Institute of Ecosystem Studies for my residency in Millbrook, NY. Your time and expertise gave inspiration to this work. My gratitude, too, to the illimitable Bryan Giemza and the Sowell Collection for extending their warm support.

I extend my gratitude to the Poetry Foundation, whose Ruth Lilly Poetry Fellowship made it possible to live and work in

Mexico's Upper Gulf of California. And to the Kate Tufts Poetry Award, the Levis Reading Prize, and the Arizona Commission on the Arts, which have supported the writing of this book.

Endless gratitude to Colin Cheney—your scintillating mind and superlative editorial deftness made this a far better book. And our Friday-morning crew: Colin, Cate Marvin, and Jefferson Navicky, my immense gratitude for your brilliant minds and encouragement as first (and repeat) readers for many of these essays. I'd go to the moon for you.

I am deeply grateful to Heather Green, Natalie Bryant, and Akiko Sekihata for their careful reading and tuning of this book. And to Van C. Gessel, Michael Brown, and Steven Kohl for their warm responses to my inquiries and insights as scholars and translators. I will always be grateful to Noriko Mizuta Lippit, Kyoko Iriye Selden, Geraldine Harcourt, and Phyllis Birnbaum, without whose tireless efforts championing, editing, and translating the work of many Japanese women writers, this book would not have been possible.

I am deeply thankful to Danielle Chapman, Pietro Federico, Becky Thompson, and Amy Dempsey for their help with this manuscript at various stages. Thanks to Angela Williamson Emmert for introducing me to the essay by Astrida Neimanis and Rachel Loewen Walker titled "*Weathering*: Climate Change and the 'Thick Time' of Transcorporeality."

Elizabeth Salper, poet and friend extraordinaire. David Keplinger, my soul twin. Tom Wilkening, I'll never forget that you showed up. Janice Welchert, Jill Koyama, Lilly Morales, Peggy Turk-Boyer, Rick Boyer, Alma Valdenebro, and Andy Burgess: Thank you for teaching me the power of community. My family in Tucson: Katalin Gothard, Andy Fuglevand, and the late Edith Seely; you will always be my loves. My colleagues and students at Stonecoast—you are an inspiration. Judy and

Franz Thomé—my gratitude for the hours of Lego playing and chocolate-éclair making with the kids so I could finish this book.

I'm so grateful to my teachers and mentors: Rita Dove, Alison Hawthorne Deming, Greg Orr, Charles Wright, and the late Louise Glück and Donna Swaim. And Deborah Eisenberg, your brilliance and generosity changed the trajectory of my life.

Heather Green, you are my muse. I couldn't have done this without you.

To my parents, who gave me a childhood filled with wonder. You are the most marvelous people on the planet. My brother and sister—Andy and Susan—you are my dearest friends and inspiration.

And to my darlings, Alex, Vivienne, and Theo—you are in every line of this book.

Katherine Larson is a poet, essayist, and biologist by training. Her debut collection of poems, *Radial Symmetry*, was selected by Louise Glück as winner of the Yale Series of Younger Poets. The recipient of a Ruth Lilly Fellowship and a Kate Tufts Discovery Award, she has been published in numerous literary journals including *Poetry*, *Orion*, and *AGNI*. Larson is active with organizations and artists dedicated to conservation and environmental education in the Gulf of California. She lives with her family in Tucson, Arizona.

milkweed
EDITIONS

Founded as a nonprofit organization in 1980, Milkweed Editions is an independent publisher. Our mission is to identify, nurture, and publish transformative literature, and build an engaged community around it.

We are based in Bdé Óta Othúŋwe (Minneapolis) in Mní Sota Makhóčhe (Minnesota), the traditional homeland of the Dakhóta and Anishinaabe (Ojibwe) people and current home to many thousands of Dakhóta, Ojibwe, and other Indigenous people, including four federally recognized Dakhóta nations and seven federally recognized Ojibwe nations.

We believe all flourishing is mutual, and we envision a future in which all can thrive. Realizing such a vision requires reflection on historical legacies and engagement with current realities. We humbly encourage readers to do the same.

milkweed.org

Milkweed Editions, an independent nonprofit literary publisher, gratefully acknowledges sustaining support from our board of directors, the McKnight Foundation, the National Endowment for the Arts, and many generous contributions from foundations, corporations, and thousands of individuals—our readers. This activity is made possible by the voters of Minnesota through a Minnesota State Arts Board Operating Support grant, thanks to a legislative appropriation from the Arts and Cultural Heritage Fund.

Interior design by Mike Corrao
Typeset in Adobe Jenson Pro

Adobe Jenson Pro is a digital facsimile of Nicolas Jenson's roman and Ludovico degli Arrighi's italic typefaces of the late 1400s. This modern rendition was designed by Robert Slimbach in 1996 as part of a concerted effort to revitalize important historical typefaces.